DETOUR

MY JOURNEY FROM
HIGH-POWERED ATTORNEY TO
AUTO MECHANIC TRADE SCHOOL
AND THE HARD TRUTHS LEARNED ALONG THE WAY

DAVID W. ELLIS

Publishing services provided by 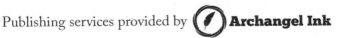 Archangel Ink

ISBN: 978-1-950043-08-8

To Hope and Madi

Go confidently in the direction of your dreams!
Live the life you've imagined.

–Henry David Thoreau

CONTENTS

INTRODUCTION

"Did you hear the alarm go off?"

Uh-oh. My instructor stands next to me and looks over my work. I had just called him over to show him that I had finished on time. It is our lab final for my Brakes course and one of the tests is to disassemble and reassemble a drum brake trainer in less than ten minutes.[1] I struggled to finish on time. I knew I was cutting it close, but I was certain I had beaten the clock. The instructor periodically called out the time remaining as three of us hovered over our individual drum brake trainers. I vaguely recall hearing "One minute left" and "Thirty seconds left"—then nothing.

"No, I did not hear it go off," I reply, not sure what would happen next. *Did the alarm in fact go off before I finished? Is he going to fail me?* I hold my breath. My hands are shaking, as they sometimes do when I'm nervous. I had known this lab final, coming on the next-to-last day of the course, was going to be a tough one for me. I had practiced on the trainer all week, but I never did reassemble the drum brake trainer in practice without another student's help. I had dreaded taking this test, but there was no way out. I had to take it. Sure enough, two minutes after starting the test, the small parts

---

1 A drum brake trainer is used for teaching the component parts of a drum-brake system on a car. It is a full-scale replica of an automobile drum brake system for one wheel of a car except, instead of being on a car, it is mounted on a stand, so you can work on it at a table.

started to slip out of my hands, and I lurched into a full-blown panic. The hardest parts are the two hold-down springs—one on each side of the trainer. Every time I thought I had them securely in the trainer, they sprung out. At one point I even had to chase an errant one across the floor like a cat toy. *How embarrassing! And everyone in the class is watching. Arrgh! Why is this so hard?* My friends go uncharacteristically quiet. Perhaps they are thinking that this time Ellis will fail the lab final. *This time, Ellis, the guy with a 4.0 GPA, is going down!*

"Well, at least you put everything back in the right place," the instructor concedes as he inspects my brake drum trainer. He then turns and walks off without another word. He does not tell me I *failed*, but then he does not tell me I *passed* either. I cautiously approach one of my friends, hoping he can confirm that I had indeed finished under the wire. He says, "I think you got it. I saw you put the last spring on at the same time the alarm was sounding." That is NOT reassuring, but there is nothing I can do or say now to change the outcome. It is entirely up to the instructor to determine whether I pass or fail. *Not my finest hour*, I think.

I have to wait for scores to be posted the following week before I learn the results from my lab final. Imagine my surprise when I find out that not only did I pass, but the instructor gave me a perfect 10!

Sweet! I breathe a sigh of relief. *I got this! (Phantom high five).*

From July 2018 until June 2019, I was a full-time student at Universal Technical Institute (UTI). I enrolled in the Automotive Technology program, which consists of seventeen three-week courses covering a wide variety of topics, including not only brakes but also automotive electronics, manual and automatic transmissions, engine management, fuel systems, ignition systems, emissions, air-conditioning, and the like. UTI is a for-profit technical school, and it offers auto-related programs at thirteen different campuses across the United States.[2] Unlike many community colleges and other schools that teach automobile repair and technology with classes meeting only once or several times a week, UTI offers full-time programs.[3] Classes meet every weekday. Since I wanted to learn as much as I could, as quickly as possible, UTI became my first choice. And I was in luck because there was a UTI campus in my metropolitan area.

Before I attended UTI, I knew precious little about how cars work and had no prior training or experience repairing a car. In this regard, I imagine I am like millions of other people who own a car or have driven cars since they were old enough to get a driver's license. I had always been an avid car aficionado who read car magazines and clicked through countless gearhead videos on YouTube, but I did not know or understand much about the various systems on a car, what they do, how they work, and why.

Before I enrolled in UTI, I had never attended a technical school. I never even took "auto shop" classes in high school. Other than spending a few summers cutting down trees for the local Forestry Department, I'd never worked with hand tools or power tools before,

---

2   According to a recent annual report, UTI's parent company is the leading provider of postsecondary education for students seeking careers as professional automotive, diesel, collision repair, motorcycle, and marine technicians—as well as welders and CNC machining technicians—as measured by total average full-time enrollment and graduates. It offers certificate, diploma, or degree programs at its thirteen campuses across the United States under the banner of several well-known brands, including UTI, Motorcycle Mechanics Institute, Marine Mechanics Institute, and NASCAR Technical Institute. Additionally, it offers manufacturer-specific advanced training programs, including student-paid electives, at its campuses, and it provides manufacturer or dealer-sponsored training at certain campuses and dedicated training centers. For the year ended September 30, 2018, the average full-time enrollment for all affiliated schools was 10,418.

3   UTI Annual Report for the fiscal year ended September 30, 2018, filed on SEC Form 10-K on November 30, 2018, page 2.

nor learned a skilled trade job—and none of my family or friends had either. I had no way to anticipate what my year at UTI would be like. My personal mantra is "Be prepared." I am the kind of person who exhaustively researches a subject, has not only a *Plan B* but a *Plan C*, and makes sure every angle is covered. I approached technical school with the same intensity. I read the promotional brochures, peppered the school admissions officer with questions, watched marketing videos prepared by the school, read the Yelp reviews, read the school's latest annual report, and gleaned what I could from a school tour for prospective students. Despite all of these efforts to do my due diligence, I was still largely unprepared. I jumped into the deep end of the pool but had no idea how to swim, how deep the water was, what temperature the water was, or how to get myself out of the pool.

Having successfully completed the one-year program, I am now a different person in several meaningful ways. First, I learned a lot about how cars work and how to repair them. Some of the technological advances in today's cars are pretty amazing and cool, and I now understand and appreciate them. The Automotive Technology program at UTI is just a basic program, however, and it does not convert neophytes like me into a Master Tech over seventeen courses. Still, with the knowledge and training I gained in this program, I can now walk into any dealership or repair shop and apply for a job as an auto technician. I am also much more confident about working on my own car and more effective in helping friends and neighbors diagnose problems with their cars.

In addition, I learned many fascinating, surprising, and—in some cases—disturbing features about the service and repair side of the automobile industry. There are a number of inherent tensions and dynamics that exist with respect to the service department at dealerships and independent shops, especially the very unusual compensation system that is designed to pay technicians at a flat rate per job, thereby putting a premium on completing a task as quickly as possible.

I also learned a great deal about the students who attend UTI—especially the financial challenges they experience while going to school. I met people who are vastly different from me, both as to background and as to age, and I became sensitized to the plight of those who survive from "hand to mouth" and are seeking to make a better life for themselves.

And I learned a lot about myself and how I respond under pressure. I am embarrassed to admit it, but I approached UTI with a sense that, even though I knew precious little about automotive technology, my academic background and my successful career to date would permit me to master a new skill set easily and proficiently. I thought, *It's technical school. How hard could it be?* I was confident that I would sail through my courses. *Boy oh boy, was I wrong!* Just because you can read and write does not mean you can become an expert in diagnosing and repairing cars in just a few months. I was humbled by the experience, and I am a better man because of it.

In short, while UTI is not a four-year liberal arts college, it provided me with the technical school equivalent of a world-class education. While it may not be the logical path for most auto enthusiasts, it was the perfect fit for me.

Here is my story.

My first day of auto tech school

Photo by Madi Ellis | madiellisphotography.com

CHAPTER 1

WHAT AM I DOING HERE?

I am not your typical UTI student. I started UTI at the tender age of sixty-two. I left my high-powered job to learn how to work on cars—something that not many people do and not a typical career path. Previously, I was a partner for almost thirty years in one of the largest international law firms in the world. I worked my way up the ranks, from associate to senior associate to partner, over the course of my career at the firm. I paid my dues by working all hours. I arrived at the office early, stayed late, and worked on weekends (both Saturdays and Sundays). I loved the practice of law both from an intellectual, problem-solving standpoint and from a client-facing standpoint. It was incredibly exciting for me, especially when it came to team projects like working on an international transaction with assets and employees spanning dozens of countries.

Although it was hard work, I really enjoyed all aspects of my practice. My specialty was cross-border employment and employee benefits. I emailed clients and colleagues in countries all over the world on a daily basis. I had a sizeable client list, an extensive network of colleagues, and friends at my home office and at other firm offices across the globe. I travelled frequently, chalking up over a hundred thousand miles in flight annually. I served on firm committees, was elected to prestigious practice leadership positions, and actively participated on various compensation committee within the firm, helping determine what all the partners would be paid. I was a frequent speaker and author on issues related to international employee compensation, and flew all over the world to give PowerPoint presentations to clients and lawyers on various emerging topics and changes in the law. I developed a series of sixty-second videos on international topics, which we named the "Global Mobility Minute," and helped with developing scripts and filming. It was a heady time, and I *loved* it. I thought that being an international lawyer was the greatest job in the world. And in return, I was "making bank," as they say. *I was living the dream.*

However, several years ago the practice of law at my firm started to change. In search of higher profits per partner, management implemented a painful process of cutting costs, letting people go, and engaging in endless reorganizations. The changes were dramatic, and they started to grate on me. In part because I had once been in management, I found myself at odds with the new management team, not only as to direction but, in particular, as to style. They were doing things I would never do. What was once a collegial, friendly place to work had lost its character. A firm that once prided itself on "the culture of friendship" was becoming more cutthroat and mercenary.

In addition, after I stepped down from my management role, I found it was an uphill battle to generate work for myself and for other people. Having handed off work and clients to others in the past, I was now expected to build my practice back up. *Not an easy task.* As I was measured strictly by these metrics and not by any "off the time sheet" contributions, such as mentoring young associates, managing clients who were unhappy because of delays in their projects, serving as a subject matter expert, or promotional and marketing efforts, I became increasingly stressed and not particularly happy. People I respected left the firm for greener pastures or were asked to step down and take lower-tier partnership positions within the firm. There was a lot of political maneuvering that accompanied these changes. I found it increasingly taxing to react to each announced internal change, one after another, on an almost weekly basis. Eventually, I stopped reading the "all hands" management-issued emails because they always raised more questions than they answered. I found myself alone—or in some cases part of a minority—in the thinking that we as a firm were making mistakes in how we should run our business, with no ability to influence any change. My former role as a member of senior management did not count for much anymore.

Management began closely monitoring my progress and eventually asked me to change my status from an equity partner to a non-equity partner to reflect the downturn in my book of business. This shift meant I was no longer going to be a member of the "club," that is, an "owner" of the business. I was no longer going to be eligible for firm leadership positions and was no longer at the top of the pyramid. It also meant I was going to make less money, but that did not really bother me. Believe it or not, I never did obsess over compensation when I was a lawyer. That was never my underlying motivation, to make as much money as possible. Instead, my motivation was to learn new aspects of the law, have fun while doing so, and leave the firm a better place than it was when I first started there. Case in point: Many of my roles within the firm were uncompensated positions which required a significant time commitment. I was always the one to "take one for the firm," such as volunteering for roles within our office and the firm that involved a lot of non-billable time. I even agreed to continue in a senior management position for an extra year when my successor was unable to take over at the end of my term. *No good deed goes unpunished*, I thought.

So when management asked me to change status, I was not happy. I was miffed that they would turn on me, especially since I had given so much of my own time to the firm during my legal career because it was the right thing to do. But I understood why they were asking me

to step down. It was a financial decision, as well as an assessment on
their part that I could not "cut it" anymore. To be honest, I had seen
it coming—if only as a reflection of my own disenchantment with the
direction of the firm. It was true, I was not growing, and practicing
law was no longer fun. The firm I had once known and loved was now
a different place to work. I decided not to fight it or make a stink.
I agreed with management that it was time to make a change, but
the change I wanted to make was more drastic than what they were
proposing. I did not want to stick around. I could not stomach being
in the back seat and just going along for the ride. I loved being in the
driver's seat. And if I couldn't do that, I was going to leave.

So I did. In the spring of 2018, I decided to retire from the firm
and do something else with my life. At the time, I thought of the
famous line, "If you're going to be run out of town on a rail, lead the
parade."[4] That's what I was going to do: leave with my head held
high. But what *exactly* was I going to do? To figure this out, I adopted
the same approach I used when I counseled any number of younger
associates who were unhappy and were thinking about leaving the
firm. I asked myself: *What is it that I like to do most? What interests me
and what makes me happy?* I came up with two answers: (1) music and
(2) cars. I have always been keenly interested in all forms and types
of music, both as a performer and as an audience. I learned how to
play the piano, flute, and guitar as a child. Everyone in my family,
including my parents, played a musical instrument. I attended the
National Music Camp in Interlochen, Michigan, for four summers
during my childhood. I studied flute in high school and college and
took lessons from a very famous flautist in Paris during my junior year
abroad. *Yes, I have music in my blood.* But what kind of career could

---

4   Interview with Gene Ellerson, football coaching aide at the University of
Miami, *Daily Herald* (Big Spring, Texas), "Looking 'em Over" with Tommy Hart,
July 2, 1957, page 7B, col. 1.

I possibly have with music? It did not take me long to concede: *No, music was NOT going to be my next career.*

And then I thought about cars. I have always been fascinated with cars—especially sports cars, in all of their variations. As a young boy, I was attracted to sports cars because they were sleek, shiny, and fast. I grew up in the muscle car era of the 60s and 70s, and there was no end to the number of Chevy Corvettes, Dodge Chargers, or Ford Mustangs for me to drool over. I knew nothing of transmissions, gear ratios, or tire grip. I was fixated on high horsepower, fast 0–60 mph times, and screaming-loud colors—especially bright red. Once I started college, I met students from wealthy families who owned expensive cars that stood out from the rest. My friends' cars included a Pontiac Trans Am, a highly modified GTO with a cool-looking engine air intake sticking out of the hood, and a BMW 2002 tii. The beautiful lines and sinuous curves of the high-end and sporty cars my friends owned would stop me dead in my tracks and make me stare.

Even today as I walk down the street, I look at cars. I routinely check out the cars parked on the street or driving by, noting which ones are brand new, which ones are kept clean, which ones are hybrid or electric, which ones have curb rash on their wheels or scratches and dents, and which ones have been tastefully modified with after-market parts so they look better than stock. My attention to these details started at a young age. Over time, I developed the ability to identify cars quickly—even when they are whizzing by or at a distance—because I looked for telltale features, such as the shape of their taillights or the contours of the front grill. When I am behind the wheel, I am pretty good at identifying the make and model of the car behind me by just glancing in my rearview mirror.

I cringe when I see a car with a lot of physical damage or rust. I wonder whether the car, if it were alive, might be embarrassed that its owner drives it looking like that. If I see a car I really like, and a driver is in it, I tell him or her, "Nice car!" *Yes, I am one of those guys.*

I once overheard a conversation between two women walking down the street. One woman said to the other, "Guys are so superficial! All a guy wants is another guy to tell him he has a nice car." I remember chuckling to myself as I heard that comment because it sounded so ludicrous. But having grown up as a "car guy," in all honesty, I think there is a lot of truth to that statement. I know how pumped I feel when another guy compliments me on my own car. I don't know if I would call if "superficial," but I now believe that the woman's observation is right on the money. The message I get is that my car is an object of desire, and to hear it confirmed by someone else is such an ego boost!

My father was a car lover at heart. We always had two cars: one for my dad and one for my mom. My dad religiously purchased a new car every three years. He was a GM man and, over the course of his life, he owned a number of different GM makes and models, with a particular affinity for Oldsmobiles. I remember he drove a Ninety-Eight, a Cutlass, and a slew of other models. In 1966, he bought an Olds Toronado, which I learned at UTI was one of the first cars to have front-wheel drive. In 1969, he purchased a green Olds 442, a car I would drive to college my sophomore year and ultimately purchase from my dad. The Olds 442 was *incredibly* fast! My dad liked to say that it had "great pickup." The Olds 442 had an eight-track cassette player in the center console. My dad had only two eight-track tapes in that car. One was a collection of songs by Herb Albert and the Tijuana Brass and the other was a collection of songs by Liberace *(don't ask)*. The Olds 442 was my favorite car. I regret that I had to sell it when I did. I never thought of it as a "chick magnet"; to me, it was just a fun car to drive. All you had to do was step on the gas and the thing would take off like a rocket! My very first fender bender (and come to think of it, my very last one) was in that car. I was in college at the time. I misjudged the distance when I was parallel parking and ended up scraping the rear quarter panel of the 442 on the back bumper of the car I was parking behind. A rookie mistake, I know, and I could have cried when it happened. That beautiful green sheet metal was horribly mangled. The local body shop was a lifesaver! In no time the car was as good as new.

My mom once had a yellow 1960 Ford Thunderbird. It had an ingenious convertible top that dropped down into the trunk. The convertible had a mechanism in which the trunk lid would open from the back and the convertible top would fold down neatly into the trunk so the trunk lid could close over it. The whole process took about sixty seconds and seemed a wonder of automation at the time. I remember that we would always draw a crowd of gawkers whenever Mom pulled over to open the convertible top. I also remember my mom once owned a beautiful red Cadillac El Dorado with a white interior. The El Dorado resembled a huge motorboat, dominating the lane. It definitely garnered a lot of attention whenever we drove in it.

I also love race cars. I raced cars briefly with a local car club but someone else always worked on the cars and repaired them. My experience racing cars was a singularly significant time in my life. I was doing well enough at the firm that I could afford to buy a Porsche 911, albeit an older one (1989) that had some mileage on it. The local Porsche club offered opportunities to take the car to a road course (one with left- and right-hand turns, changes in elevation, straights, curves, etc.) and learn how to drive it safely at high speeds on the track. I was nervous the first time I went out with a driving instructor (someone like me, who worked full-time but owned a Porsche and drove it in his spare time), but I was also incredibly excited! The instructor's helmet had a built-in microphone and headset that was paired with a similar set built into my helmet. We could easily talk to each other at a regular volume over the noise of the car's engine, as well as the noise from all the other cars on the track. The instructor talked me through the basics of driving at speed, where to brake, when to shift, how to look for the corner workers with their flags and follow their instructions, and how to treat the car so it would deliver performance for me—and not kill me. That first time I sat in the driver's seat of a Porsche when driving on a track (with the instructor in the passenger seat) was an incredible high! I grinned from ear-to-ear throughout the drive, even when I made minor mistakes such as braking too early or too late, going off-line, or even going off the track. It was a pure adrenaline rush, driving the car at speed on a track. I can think of nothing that approaches the sensation, the sound of the engine and the wind rushing by the vehicle, and the ability to accelerate hard, brake hard, and control a car through a corner. I was hooked! Nothing could come close to the sheer joy I felt whenever I was behind the wheel of a race car.

My love affair with driving fast on the track soon morphed into club racing, an amateur event where I raced my car against other Porsches of the same vintage, with similar engines and weight, under the auspices of the Porsche Club of America. I travelled all over the country and raced at some of the most famous road courses in the United States, such as Sebring, Mid-Ohio, Watkins Glen, Road Atlanta, and Road America. I was by no means the fastest driver on the track. On the contrary, I was actually one of the slowest. It is indeed a humbling experience to be one of the last drivers across the finish line in a race. I was often passed several times during the race by faster cars and more accomplished drivers. I always saw other drivers receive awards for first, second, and third place. As you can imagine, the fastest drivers are heroes in the club racing scene and are treated like minor celebrities. Some of them are real assholes both on the track and off it, but many of them are charming, humble, friendly, and genuinely nice guys. It takes some skill to be a good racer. Everyone initially thinks it is easy, but I can attest it is much harder than it looks. Before I began racing I would watch various races on television and conclude, *I can do that*. The televised footage is deceptive: Cars seem to glide smoothly and seamlessly around the track. Even when there is a camera inside the car showing the viewing audience the cockpit and controls, the driver appears almost immovable, relying on seemingly minute movements to steer the car. He or she hardly seems to break a sweat, and driving looks effortless. But when it is you inside the race car—accelerating, shifting gears, braking, turning at the right time, dealing with the noise, reacting to the g-forces on your body as the car moves around the track (they are the most brutal, by the way, when you are braking hard), and avoiding other drivers—it is by no means an easy feat. I used to tell people that when you are driving a race car at speed on a road course, it might look easy from the spectator's viewpoint, but inside the car it is *violent*. My own race car was an older car by today's standards. It had no power steering, no power brakes, no ABS, and no air-conditioning. It was always hot and loud, and at the end of every race I was soaked with sweat and thoroughly exhausted. After some particularly hot and grueling races, I unbuckled my safety belts and literally crawled out of the car on my hands and knees. *But I loved it!* I loved being on the track with other racers. I loved comparing notes with the other racers in my group on race strategy and track conditions, and sharing ideas for going faster. So I kept at it, telling myself that over time I was going to get better, that experience would help me get faster, and that there is no shortcut. I had to just go out there and try my best, and eventually I would become a faster racer.

Unfortunately, my racing days were cut short by a horrific accident. At one particular track, I braked hard going into a "carousel," a long curving section of the track that is usually taken a little slower and where the tire grip often becomes an issue because of the curving pavement. I stepped hard on the brake pedal as I entered the carousel, but instead of feeling resistance, as I had on the prior corner, there was no resistance and the brake pedal went all the way to the floor. I had no brakes, so the car went off the track and headed straight for a grove of trees. It all happened in a fraction of a second. I don't remember the impact, but I do recall opening my eyes immediately after impact. The front of the car had wrapped itself around a small tree. Luckily, the windshield had not shattered and there was no fire (in this car, the engine is in the rear). I suddenly felt an intense shooting pain in my lower back. It literally took my breath away. I had to unbuckle my racing safety belts and exit the car through the passenger side, as the driver's side door was wedged against a tree, making it impossible for me to open the door—or even climb out the driver's side window. I could barely walk when the safety team arrived, and I was taken to the hospital in an ambulance. The X-rays showed several compression fractures in my lower back. The orthopedic surgeon put me in a clamshell-style back brace for several months, and I endured months of physical therapy afterwards. I never fully healed and my back is permanently injured. It hurts when I sit too long, especially on airplanes (where I need a pillow for the small of my back). I have since resigned myself to enduring some back pain for the rest of my life. Sitting for more than an hour or two without standing up and stretching will always be a problem for me.

As a result of my accident, I gave up racing altogether. I sold what was left of the race car (the front was a gnarled mess, pancaked to the dashboard, making the vehicle resemble a golf cart more than a race car) and gave away all of my race gear. I was ashamed and embarrassed that I had crashed my car the way I had, but there was no going back. When I arrived home from the hospital after my accident, my wife and daughter confronted me about the dangers of racing and made me swear I would never *ever* get behind the wheel again. There were lots of tears all around. I promised them I would never drive a race car again.

But it still was one of the greatest times of my life. Racing is a visceral thrill. If you have never driven a car at speed on a racetrack, I encourage you to do so. *You will not regret it.* It is literally *life in the fast lane* (apologies to the Eagles). I'll never drive on the track again, but the memories endure. I still have a love affair with racing and race cars.

But other than those limited experiences, I never worked on a car, nor knew much about how cars worked. No one in my family was a mechanic or worked on cars as a hobby. In fact, none of my childhood friends knew much about cars either. I admit, despite my love for them, cars for me were a "black box." Like many people, I possessed no more than a passing knowledge and general notions based on my observations from driving. I knew cars were complex, but I really did not know in what way—or how to appreciate the engineering or complexity. When my car needed a repair, I would take it to a dealer who would install me in a waiting room while the car disappeared behind a wall into the garage to be worked on by a total stranger. After an hour (or *two* . . . or *three*) the car, newly washed, was driven to the front of the dealership by a porter and pronounced "fixed." I probably could have/should have asked more questions along the way. At a minimum, I probably should have read the owner's manual. After all, cars are pretty expensive and as the owner I should have known a lot more about what makes them run. But I remained blissfully ignorant. The car was a "black box" and I was okay with that, at least for a while.

I did make one attempt to "hot rod" my dad's Olds 442. It was the year I had the car at college. For some reason, I thought I could make the car go even faster if I put a Holley carburetor on the engine. I cannot recall how I knew anything about Holley carburetors, but I do recall my dad had a subscription to *Car and Driver*, so maybe that's where I saw an ad for them. I went to a local auto parts store and asked the man behind the counter if he could order a Holley carburetor for the 442. He looked it up in a catalog the size of a Merriam-Webster dictionary—unabridged—and asked me what size carburetor I wanted. The particular details of our exchange are blurry, but somehow I ended up getting one that was rated at 650 CFM (cubic feet per minute: the maximum volume of air the carburetor allows to be sucked into the engine).

The day I picked up the new carburetor, I naively thought that it would be a relatively easy unbolt/bolt-on kind of project. I borrowed some tools from a friend of mine, consisting of a screwdriver, a hammer (?), and a pair of pliers. That was about it. There might have been some instructions with the new Holley carburetor, I don't recall. But I do recall that it took me forever to figure out what to remove, what to install, etc. Throughout the day, several of my friends dropped by to see how I was coming along. Since I had no idea what I was doing, I asked everyone for advice. By the time we finished, there must have been four or more of us crowded around, hanging over the car fenders and looking into the engine.

Sufficiently assured the carburetor was successfully installed, I fired up the engine. *Uh-oh.* Something was wrong. The engine did not idle smoothly and began to hesitate and sputter. I tried gunning the engine a little to see if that would help. It did not. Imagine the scene of four college guys staring blankly at a sputtering engine, wondering what to do next. *Insert joke here.*

After turning off the ignition and sparing my poor 442 any further torture, I had an idea. If I could coax my car to a service station, a mechanic might be able to diagnose what was causing my new carburetor to sputter. I made it to the nearest service station and convinced the mechanic (for $20) to look at the engine and see if he could fix it. He tried valiantly for an hour, but could not figure out the problem. I started to get a little panicky and thought that maybe I was going to be stuck with an engine that did not run smoothly. Before I did that, however, I had one more idea. *Perhaps the issue is with the Holley 650!* So I drove the sputtering car to the auto parts store and found the guy who had sold me the new carburetor.

"This thing doesn't work," I told him. I explained how I had installed the carburetor, described the problem I was having, and told him that I had taken the car to a mechanic at a gas station to fix the problem, but the engine was still hesitating and sputtering.

"Oh," said the guy at the counter, "you're in luck because there is a very good mechanic here in the store right now." He pointed out a man standing in line at the cash register. "He was once the crew chief for Richard Petty's race team.[5] Perhaps he can help you out."

After introductions were made, the three of us trooped out to my car, which was sitting in the parking lot. I opened the hood and started up the engine. The Former Crew Chief For Richard Petty looked at the engine for . . . *maybe* . . . two seconds, pointed to a small hole in the engine right below the carburetor, and declared matter-of-factly, "There's a bolt missing from the intake manifold. You have a vacuum leak."

I sheepishly pulled out of my pocket a bunch of parts that I had taken off the car and said, "Oh. Must be one of these. I was not sure what to do with these extra parts."

The Former Crew Chief For Richard Petty took one of the bolts out of my hand, screwed it into the small opening with his fingers, and . . . *Voila!* The engine . . . ran . . . perfectly. It just *hummed*. No more hesitation. No more sputter. He had fixed it just like that.

I remembered that story as I was contemplating my future after law. I thought to myself, *I want to be able to do that! I want to be able to listen to a sputtering engine, point to a hole in the intake manifold, and tell a silly college student that his engine has a vacuum leak. I want to be THAT GUY.*

So I decided I would learn how to fix cars. And to do that, I would go to school to learn the basics from the ground up. You should have seen the look on my wife's face when I told her the next chapter of my life was going to start with a year at automotive technical school to learn how to wrench on cars. It was priceless.

I received an equally puzzled, if not downright skeptical, look

---

5   Richard Petty is one of the most famous NASCAR race drivers of all time.

from my friends at the firm and from my clients. I was honest with them. I told them I wanted to learn something new and to have fun. Most of them had no idea how to respond when I told them I was headed to automotive technical school. I got a lot of strange looks. Many people thought I was joking, like I had just proclaimed that I was going to become an astronaut or climb Mount Everest. At lunch one day, a group of clients collectively suggested I go by the name "Big Dave" at school and have it stitched onto my uniform so I would fit in. Another client asked me if going to technical school meant I was going to get a tattoo.[6]

Of course, all of this kidding was good-natured, so I did not mind it. I was absolutely certain that I was headed in the right direction. It was something I wanted to do. Several other friends and clients I told were much more positive and supportive about my new direction. A few of them expressed sincere jealousy that I had the time and inclination to leave my profession of over thirty years and learn how to work on cars. One friend who likes cars but never has time to work on them exclaimed, "You're my hero!" Well, I don't proclaim to be anyone's hero, but once I decide to do something, I do it.

---

6   Another client simply could not get her head around it and just kept repeating over and over that she could not understand why I would give up a "high-powered job as a senior partner" to attend technical school. I like to think that was her way of saying she was really going to miss me.

CHAPTER 2

BASIC ENGINES

It is Monday, July 2, 2018, 6:30 AM. I am seated in a classroom with twenty-nine other aspiring auto technicians, ready to begin my education. My alarm went off at 4:30 AM so I could shower, dress, and drive to the UTI campus in time for class. Getting up at 4:30 AM is not my idea of fun, especially since as a lawyer I considered myself a night owl and often saw midnight before I went to bed. But since I had enrolled in the morning program at UTI, I had to get up super early in order to make it to class on time. On the plus side, class would be over at 12:45 PM, leaving me the rest of the day to study, relax, or do whatever I wanted.

All of us are dressed in the school uniform: UTI shirt (tucked in), jeans or work pants without holes, ID badges visible at all times, no hats, and work shoes or boots with oil-resistant and slip-resistant soles. I glance around the classroom and see young faces of all colors and races. In this class, as in almost all of my classes at UTI, there is a great deal of racial and ethnic diversity—but there are no women.

I am very excited to be in school and starting off my new career. Over the next few weeks and months, my enthusiasm for school and learning will get me through the rigors of my new early morning schedule. I feel like a kid again. It's as if someone has waved a magic wand and has given me the chance to "go back to school" in the way that my college friends and I speculated at our twenty-fifth reunion. We mused about how much fun it would be to go back to college, knowing what we know now. But in this case, I am all alone in this endeavor. No college buddies—or any buddies, for that matter—are taking classes with me. I am entirely on my own and nobody knows who I am or where I came from. And I love it!

Our instructor, Mr. M[7], is an outgoing, friendly guy with a wicked sense of humor. He has lots of funny stories to tell about his years in the field as an auto technician before coming to UTI to teach. He also has a very good handle on how to engage the incoming class of students. He takes the time to explain everything in basic terms and handles every question he is asked. He also has some unique pet peeves. For example, he does not like the expression "my bad" and told us he thought it was a cowardly way of saying, "Sorry, I made a mistake." He forbade us from using that expression in class and made fun of anyone who said it. We quickly learned to stop using it.

Every UTI student studying automotive technology begins with the same class, entitled Automotive Engines and Repair. We just called it Basic Engines for short. Given that Mr. M often teaches the Basic Engines course at this school, it means that he is the first instructor—and the first face of UTI—for many of the new students.[8] Basic Engines, like every course at UTI, is a three-week course. Classes take place Monday through Friday. At the end of the course, students are tested on the material in two ways: a lab final (taking measurements and other hands-on tests) and a final exam (twenty multiple-choice questions). Assuming you pass the course,

---

7   In the interest of protecting everyone's privacy, I am using initials only for the instructors and fake names (aliases) for the students.

8   Mr. M often teaches Basic Engines in both the morning and afternoon sessions, which is extremely time-consuming and leaves him little— if any—time for family, except on weekends. He was one of the few instructors who wanted to double course. Instructors who double course get paid more, naturally.

the following Monday you start another course on another topic in another classroom with another instructor. That's the way the schedule goes for all seventeen courses in the Automotive Technology program. Students who enroll in additional programs, such as an advanced manufacturer-specific training program, may end up taking up to twenty-five or more courses.

UTI is very strict about its dress code, its focus on attendance, and its emphasis on professionalism. If you are out of uniform, you get an infraction. If you are late, you get an infraction. If you are caught using your cell phone in class (they must be put away when the bell rings), smoking on campus, fighting (on campus or in the parking lot), or bullying someone, you get an infraction. If you are caught sleeping in class, you get an infraction; and if you were previously warned about not sleeping in class, you might even be dismissed for the day and sent home, depending on the instructor. You are allowed only a certain number of infractions before you fail the course. And failure means you must retake the course (and pay more money to the school for extra tuition).

On the first day of Basic Engines, we spent the entire day doing introductory-type tasks. Mr. M passed out the course materials (three-hole punched, to be inserted into our blue UTI binders), which largely mirrored the various lectures he would present during the course. This process was replicated by every instructor on the first day of every course. Mr. M also passed out a red Course Book that was massive. It covered everything we would learn in the entire program (all seventeen courses) and was entitled *Automotive Service: Inspection – Maintenance – Repair*, by Tim Gilles (5th Edition, 2016).[9] This book was by far the heaviest schoolbook I have ever owned. It is the size and weight of a large dictionary. It rivals the dimensions of many coffee table art books. It contains 82 chapters, 1758 pages,

9   Referred to as "Course Book."

and weighs 9.3 pounds. Because I carried it to school in my backpack almost every day, by the end of the year I had noticeably built up my arm and shoulder muscles. *Really*. The information in this Course Book is incredibly detailed and invaluable. Lectures for each and every course, including pictures of components and systems (with a few exceptions), were taken directly from the material in this book. The Course Book was written exclusively for UTI and most of the contributing reviewers are UTI s, including many of the instructors I had during my year there. The Course Book has self-study questions that are the basis for some of our test questions, so reading the assigned chapters and doing the self-study questions was extremely helpful.

One activity that occurs on the first day of every course is called "SOPs" (an acronym for "Standard Operating Procedures"). SOPs is a presentation on the school's policies: the *do's* and *don'ts* of attending UTI and guidelines on how to behave in class. For example, during the SOPs you are reminded about all of the things you are not supposed to do in class and all the things that may land you an infraction, such as violation of the uniform, attendance, or professionalism rules. During the SOPs, you are reminded that you must take a hall pass and leave your ID in class to go the bathroom (*but don't take too long—that could merit another infraction!*). In addition, SOPs cover emergency procedures: where to go in the event of a fire or tornado and what to do in the case of an active shooter. They also outline general school policies. Some of these policies seem to be almost born of necessity at a school where everyone drives to campus every day. You are reminded that there is no speeding in the parking lot, that burnouts and "donuts" are not permitted in the parking lot, and that you must obey all local speed limits on the roads leading up to the school, as UTI students tend to speed (*surprise!*) and neighbors have complained. Depending on the instructor, SOPs can take anywhere from twenty minutes to two hours. Each instructor also uses this opportunity to give the class a little of his own background: where he has worked, what types of cars he has worked on, why he might have moved from one job to another, and how he landed as an instructor at UTI. Some instructors, like Mr. M, have decades of experience in the field before teaching at UTI. Other younger instructors may spend as few as ten to fifteen years in the field before they start teaching at UTI. I don't know how much money UTI instructors make, but from what they told us, it sounded like it was not a lot of money but it also was not chump change. A few of my instructors did in fact leave UTI during my year to return to the field and work. I suspect that the attraction of more money was a big reason why they left.

On that first day, Mr. M did an activity with us that we never repeated in any other course. He had each of us stand up and introduce our table partner to the rest of the class. This is an "icebreaker" exercise with which I am well acquainted. I did it several times as a lawyer when attending various sensitivity workshops and HR training sessions. Mr. M dubbed it "Getting to Know You." Before we started, he clicked on a file in his computer to play the song "Getting to Know You" from the Broadway show *The King and I*. Everyone was rolling their eyes at this corny approach. But we dutifully stood up one by one and introduced our table partners. To help everyone overcome their stage fright and jump-start the process, Mr. M handed us a list of questions we could ask our table partner during the few minutes of preparation we were given before our presentations. The questions covered basic topics such as: "What is your favorite snack? What is your favorite car? What do you like to do in your free time?" My table partner, Correda,[10] was an eighteen-year-old who had graduated from high school just a few weeks prior. He was not very talkative, but he did let on that he had taken tae kwon do classes. Most of the kids were not very confident when it came their turn to speak and there

---

10   Again, I am not using real names, only aliases.

was a lot of looking downward, reading from their notes verbatim, mumbling, and general anxiety. From the introductions, it seemed that the UTI students favored all types of cars, from older muscle cars of the 1960s and 1970s with huge horsepower engines to speedy foreign cars (e.g., "hot hatches"). A lot of their free time seemed to be devoted to playing video games and eating snack foods that were completely unknown to me. When it was my turn to introduce Correda, however, I could not pass up the opportunity to say something I thought was funny. I embellished Correda's background and said that he was a black belt in tae kwon do and was training for the Olympics—and if anyone was going to have a knife fight in an alley, they should take Correda along because he would *kick everyone's ass!* I noticed Correda out of the corner of my eye turn beet red when I said that last part. He was mortified that I had built him up and gone "off script." He tried to make himself as small as possible. The class tittered at my remarks, but Mr. M could not leave it alone. He instantly quipped, "Well, if he does that, *that* would be an infraction!" The class roared with laughter and Correda smiled a little, too. *Welcome to UTI.*

As part of the SOPs, each instructor also reviews the different subjects that will be tested during the course, how many tests will be given in each class (usually ten, but in some classes we had only eight), the number of points each test is worth (most tests were comprised of ten questions, with each question worth one point, although in some courses we had 15-question tests), the different lab sheets we must complete, a description of the lab final, and general information we need to know to pass the course. Every test is multiple choice. UTI does not use essay tests like the ones I had in college or law school. At UTI, you record your answers by filling in a bubble on a Scantron sheet with a No. 2 pencil. Each final exam in every course consists of 20 questions. In most courses, the total number of class test points add up to 100, meaning you take eight, 10-point tests and one 20-point final test.[11] Over a three-week course, you end up taking a test in class almost every other day. That is *a lot* of testing, for certain, but it also creates a rhythm. You have a lecture one day, study that night, and are then tested on the lecture material the next day. Labs typically occur on an every-other-day basis as well.

There were many unknowns when it came to lab work at UTI. The lab sheets we completed were usually due the same day as the lab assignment, but in some cases, they could be turned in later. We never really knew what work we had to do on the lab sheets until the day of the lab, when the instructor provided us with instructions on how to correctly complete it. In some courses we were told how many points each lab sheet would be worth, but in others, we did not know until we received a progress report that revealed our lab scores. What we did know, however, was that in every course, the lab final was worth 30% of your ultimate lab score. At UTI, in order to pass each course, you have to earn at least a 70% in class points (the multiple-choice tests) and a 70% in lab points. Since the lab final alone is worth 30% of your final lab score, failing the lab final often means you fail the course. This unfortunate event did occur for some students during my year at UTI. In most cases they had failed to show up to school the day of the lab final. Since the school does not allow a student to make up a missed lab final (other than in extremely unusual cases), these students consequently failed the course and had to repeat it.

If you receive the highest lab grade in the class, and at least a 90% in your class points, you earn the award of "Student of the Course" or "SOC." The names of the SOCs for all the courses are posted on a bulletin board for the entire school to see. Sometimes there was more than one SOC for each course, but usually the award was given to just one student. Each SOC is entitled to a pin that he or she can affix to

---

11   However, in some classes there were only 80 test points in total, meaning you took only six, 10-point tests and one 20-point final.

his or her ID badge. Accordingly, once the SOCs were announced at the conclusion of a course cycle, those happy students headed to a staff member in the Resource Center to receive their pins. Some students had multiple SOCs. Their ID badges were covered with so many SOC pins that you could barely see their ID badge photos.

When I started at UTI, I did not really care if I earned SOC. Mr. M mentioned that some guys would be "gunning for" SOC. I decided I would not be one of those people. My goal was to learn, not to attain the SOC award for each class. Gunning for SOC was the "old me." As a member of the Baby Boomer generation, I was taught that you have to *study, study, study* to earn top grades, compete, and get the best job. I did that when I studied to become a lawyer. However, at UTI I wanted to take a different approach. The "new me" would relax more and not focus as much on my grades. Once I committed to a yearlong study of automotive technology, I told myself that my time at UTI should not be about grades. I did not want to define myself by how many SOCs I achieved. I wanted to avoid resorting to the old competitive habits I had honed to perfection to attain success at law school and as a lawyer.

Despite these early intentions, over the course of the year I found myself changing my tune about earning SOC. Over time, the old "competitive me" inevitably emerged. I wanted to earn SOC—or at least be in the running for SOC—in every course. As I progressed through more and more courses, I found I had more in common with students who were "gunning for" SOC than I had expected. In fact, I spent most of my time with these other students. They were the smarter students in class, could explain to me things I did not understand, and were usually excellent technicians. I wanted to "hang" with this crowd. I developed a real camaraderie with this crowd over the course of the year. I admit, I also wanted the "street cred" at UTI that came with being an SOC. Other students were very aware of who had achieved SOC. It was a status symbol at the school to be SOC.

A few courses in, I definitely wanted to earn SOC in addition to just learning. I ended up with eight SOCs over my seventeen courses.[12]

Four of us comprised each lab group in Basic Engines. Every lab group was assigned a toolbox and an engine mounted on an engine stand (meaning the engine was removed from the car, making it more accessible for us to work on). Our engines were a V-8 configuration by General Motors. The engine was stripped down, consisting of the base engine parts: the block, the crankshaft, pistons, cylinder heads, the cam shaft, the harmonic balancer, the timing chain, valve covers, etc. There was no oil, coolant, gasoline or other fluids to deal with, which would have made our lab work considerably messier. We took apart the engine and rebuilt it a number of times. We measured component parts, such as the crankshaft, the cam shaft, the connecting rods for the pistons, the gaps between the piston rings and the grooves where the piston rings were seated, and the thickness of the bearings. We learned how incredibly tight the clearances were between some of the moving parts, as well as how to measure these minute clearances. It amazed me that some of the clearances are mere *thousandths* of an inch! We learned that fasteners needed to be torqued[13] down to spec, and that you must look up the specs in the manufacturer's guide or other reference materials. I learned that a torque wrench is used to measure the amount of torque applied to a fastener, and the proper method to torque a fastener. This was a whole new world of information for me. I had never seen an engine

---

12   But I never bragged about it and never requested a pin for my ID badge for the SOCs I earned. I did not want to flaunt these awards.

13   Torque is a twisting force. I learned you can use a torque wrench to measure how tightly bolts and other fasteners are twisted onto a component or into a hole. Given that heat, vibration, and other environmental factors can affect fasteners in a car engine or elsewhere on a car, it is extremely important that any fastener be tightened to the exact specification that the manufacturer has engineered for the component—no more and no less.

from this perspective before. I had arrived at UTI with no idea what all of the parts in an engine were called. In this way, I was probably similar to most new students at UTI: *I did not know what I did not know.* I even had trouble assisting with the inventory of the toolbox because I did not know the names of the individual tools. *What the hell is a valve spring compressor anyway?* I didn't even know what a valve spring was—or even what it looked like. I was soon going to find out in Basic Engines.

Not everyone in my Basic Engines class knew as little as I did. A few students arrived with varying degrees of prior experience. They had worked on engines before, either because they worked in the field as technicians or had taken auto shop in high school. A couple of them were very familiar with engines and fairly easily took them apart and put them back together. These relatively proficient students intimidated me, but I tried not to show it. I asked them questions as we went along so I could learn from them: "Why are you putting it on that way? How did you know the socket to use for that part was ⅜"?

Of course, we had a smattering of jokers in Basic Engines who really did not try very hard to learn. One of them, Valejo, was in my lab group. During labs, he was often out of the room, leaving the rest of us to carry his end of the load. You could find him either in the bathroom or in the hallway on his cell phone—despite the fact that cell phone use during class was permitted only if you received an important call, such as from a prospective employer. In those situations, permission was still required before taking out your phone, and you had to step into the hallway to conduct your conversation so as not to disturb the rest of the class. Despite this strict prohibition, Valejo seemed to be on his cell phone almost daily; and yet he very rarely asked for permission to leave the room. And I doubt his callers were prospective automotive employers. One time in lab, Valejo simply walked out while he was torquing bolts to an engine. He just handed his torque wrench to his lab partner and left. We all looked at each other quizzically and exclaimed, "WTF?" This guy really did not give a shit about the course. He was in several of my other courses, but I made certain to never again to be in his lab group. Eventually he failed a course and then he was off my cycle and no longer taking the same courses as the rest of us. I think he quit school or transferred to the afternoon program because I did not see him in the hallways after a few months.

During the first week of Basic Engines, a diminutive group of visitors trooped into our lab. A group of elementary school children was touring the school. UTI is particularly good about inviting groups for tours of the campus, especially high school groups (likely in auto shop classes). Every now and then, the tour groups consist of elementary schoolers. As they entered the lab, I overheard the guide (a UTI employee) describe to the kids what we were doing. Many of the kids wandered around the room to see us work, but they were admonished not to touch anything—*or else!* I remember thinking they must be so impressed by the room of men in school uniforms diligently working on their engines. We must have appeared very grown up and professional to them. Appearances aside, the truth was that we were just starting our education at UTI and most of us knew *jack shit* about engines. The kids didn't know that, of course, but it was odd that so early into our automotive training we were put "on display" in this way.

One time, another instructor came into the lab to talk to Mr. M. Since my lab group was assigned to work on an engine coincidentally located near the door, I could easily overhear the conversation between Mr. M and the other instructor.

The other instructor chuckled and summarily dismissed our class with, "Wait until these guys come to my class and work on *real* engines."

Mr. M shrugged. He calmly replied, "It's baby steps. You have to walk before you run."

I give Mr. M a lot of credit for defending us like that. He could have sided with the other instructor's snub and agreed, "Yeah, these guys are real dumbasses." (Which would have been accurate statement, by the way.) But he didn't say that. That other instructor was clearly a jerk. And no, I did not have him as an instructor for any of my other courses.

Mr. M really enjoyed teaching us, and he savored his lectures. He often shared personal stories involving his own working experiences or wrenching on his Corvette. He once told us a funny story about how his loudly colored vintage Corvette suffered from vapor lock on a hot day and stopped dead at an intersection. This malfunction caused a massive backup on the street, and everyone who had to drive around his stalled car yelled obscenities at him. He also often included references to his family or relayed humorous situations that occurred with other technicians over the course of his career (e.g., someone who was supposed to do an oil change on a customer's car and loosened the wrong drain plug under the engine—the one for the automatic transmission fluid *instead of the oil*).

Mr. M has taught Basic Engines so long that his lectures resemble tight comedy routines where every word is scripted. Here is an example:

Mr. M: "We need to calculate the difference between these two gear ratios. Who has a phone with a calculator?"

Valdez (sitting in the first row, eagerly whips out his phone to do the calculation and raises his hand):

"I do!"

Mr. M (with a *faux* serious glare): "You know, Valdez, taking out your phone in class is an infraction." (The class laughs.)

Valdez hurriedly puts the phone away and stares glumly ahead.

Mr. M: "No, I was just kidding with you, Valdez. It's okay. Really. It's okay. Can you do the calculation?"

Valdez cautiously takes out his phone again, ready for the numbers Mr. M wants to calculate.

Mr. M: "Hah! That's *two* infractions!"

(The class is laughing uncontrollably. Valdez fell for the joke again.)

Valdez again puts his phone away in his pocket. He is slightly mad now. He knows he is the butt of the joke.

Mr. M: "No, I was just kidding with you, Valdez. It's okay. Really."

Valdez does not move a muscle. He just stares straight ahead. He is not going to reach for his phone. *No matter what.* The fact that Valdez does not move makes the entire scene that much funnier. The class is really laughing now.

Mr. M: "C'mon, Valdez."

Valdez shakes his head no. He does not reach for his phone.

Mr. M: "You know, Valdez, failure to follow an instructor's request is also an infraction."

The class roars with laughter. Valdez is clearly confused. He turns a little red. But he does not reach for his phone in his pocket. He sits stock-still and just stares straight ahead. By now Mr. M is laughing too. He lets Valdez off the hook, though.

Mr. M: "Well, since no one seems to be able to do this very simple calculation"—he looks directly at Valdez—"I'll demonstrate this to the class myself with my own calculator . . ."

End of scene.

You might wonder how I did in Basic Engines. I aced the first three tests. They seemed fairly easy to me, but I never let on; no one likes a braggart. Also, I had diligently studied every night, reading the course materials, going over my notes, and reviewing the self-study chapters in the big red Course Book. UTI dispensed progress reports to us (aka "report cards") after every test. This immediate and consistent means for students to track their own progress is something I think that UTI does very well. Instructors routinely hand out progress reports the day after every test so everyone keeps apprised of how they are doing in the course. The progress report includes not only all of your class test scores, but also your scores on the lab sheets, your attendance record, and whether you have incurred any infractions.

As he handed me the third progress report showing my three perfect 10s, Mr. M said, "Must be pretty easy for you."

"No—" I stammered, instantly embarrassed and unsure of how to respond. "I'm just a good guesser."

Lame, I know. As it so happened, on the very next test I got one answer wrong. I decided Mr. M must have jinxed me. I am in no way superstitious, but I was now sensitive to any compliments I received from an instructor regarding my test scores. Sure enough, this scenario repeated itself in other courses. I soon became convinced that any compliment from an instructor in any course would be the "kiss of death" and would prevent me from earning a perfect 10 on the next test. It recurred at several other times during the year, including in my Automatic Transmissions course and in my Electronic Diagnostics course. A jinx is a jinx, and I wanted no part of it.

That test question I got wrong after Mr. M's unintended jinx was the only one I missed during the entire three-week course in Basic Engines. I even managed a perfect 20 on the final exam, so my class grade was a 99 out of 100. Despite my relatively high class grade, my lab final grade did not match it. During my lab final, I had trouble measuring an engine component with a dial gauge, a small measuring device with a spring-loaded plunger attached to a circular gauge. The entire contraption is held by two adjustable arms that are connected to a magnetic base. I struggled with manipulating the small, sensitive measuring device so it would stay planted at the correct angle and give an accurate reading. And, yes, the lab final was timed, so I was stressed as the clock counted down. *Sound familiar?* My grade on the lab final was a 27 out of 30. I did very well on the rest of the labs so my lab grade overall for Basic Engines was a 97. For each course at

UTI, the lab grade counts for 50% of your final grade, and the class grade counts for the other 50%. My final grade for Basic Engines was a 98 (99 + 97, divided by 2), meaning I got an A for the course.

I did not earn SOC for Basic Engines. At that point I still wasn't "gunning for" SOC, remember? I did learn an incredible amount of new information, however, much of which proved to be foundational background information for my later courses. There were plenty of "lightbulb" or *"Now I get it"* moments in Basic Engines for me. Several such "lightbulb" moments occurred when we were studying the engine's cooling system. I learned that liquid under pressure has a higher boiling point, which is why the radiator on a car boils over if you make the mistake of removing the cap while the car is still hot. The loss of pressure lowers the boiling point of the coolant and—*voila!*—the stuff just gushes out super-hot. I also learned that the "W" in the label for engine oil, (e.g., 10W-30) does not stand for "weight."[14] The guy who attained SOC was Rogers, an eighteen-year-old who earned a perfect score for the entire course. I did not know Rogers at the time, but after a couple of shared courses, we ended up sitting next to each other and made sure to join the same lab groups. I grew to know him pretty well during the year and respected his knowledge and practical experience. Rogers worked on his own cars (two Jeeps) and had studied welding in high school. We soon became fast friends.

---

14 It stands for "winter" in a multi-grade oil. The number directly before the "W" is the viscosity (thickness) of the oil at 0 degrees Fahrenheit (generally). The lower the "W" number, the thinner the oil, and the better the oil's cold temperature performance. The other number in a multi-grade oil is the oil's viscosity at 212 degrees Fahrenheit. The higher the number, the thicker the oil.

CHAPTER 3

WHO IS THAT GUY?

"What's up, Ellis?"

That was how the other students greeted me at school. We referred to each other exclusively by our last names. The instructors usually included the prefix "Mr." (or "Ms."), followed by each student's last name. This form of greeting initially seemed somewhat strange, but I soon got used to it. As a lawyer, I often called my colleagues by their *first* name and did so even with my clients (when appropriate). At UTI we *never* used first names. In fact, it was weeks or months before I learned some people's first names, and I only did so by sneaking a peek at their ID badges.

As the oldest student in the class and, with few exceptions, the oldest person in the school (two of my instructors were sixty-five and sixty-seven, respectively), I was very sensitive to the age difference between me and everyone else. During the "Getting to Know You" icebreaker in Basic Engines, I quickly picked up on the fact that almost everyone—except for one veteran and three students who had been in the field for a few years prior to enrolling at UTI—had only *just recently* graduated from high school. Accordingly, the vast majority of students in my Basic Engines course were eighteen or nineteen. I never met another student during my year at UTI who was even within twenty-five years of my age. The oldest student I met was Grossman, who was in three of my last four courses at UTI. He served for a number of years in the army and, following his discharge, worked as a corrections officer in a state prison for a number of years. Grossman has ... er ... *colorful* language honed by his various experiences. His stories of what had occurred to him during his time in the army and later, as a prison guard, were some of the most fascinating and bawdy I heard at school. Sorry, I will not repeat them here.

For better or worse, I consider myself a relatively naïve person, so I assumed— repeat, I *assumed*—that age would be the biggest differentiator between me and the other UTI students. I figured they would consider me "The Old Man" or something similarly age denigrating. I thought they might be somewhat hostile or suspicious of someone like me sitting in their classes with them, since I was clearly *old enough to be their GRANDFATHER.*

I am happy to report that my fear of being singled out as an old fuddy-duddy did not materialize. On the contrary, it took only a couple of days in Basic Engines before I felt like I was just "one of the guys." Students greeted me by my last name (like everyone else) and in some cases we fist-bumped. (The fist bump also took a little getting used to; UTI students do not shake hands with each other.) I showed up for the start of class at the ungodly hour of 6:30 AM, the same as they did. I wore the same uniform, attended the same lectures, took the same tests, laughed at Mr. M's jokes the same as they did, and struggled through the same labs. I did not stand out in any measurable way. I consciously avoided discussing my own life or any of my previous successes as a lawyer. I did not make snide remarks, funny comments, or tell stories the way the other students did. So, to most of them I was just an older fellow. While a few of my classmates may have dismissed me as an outsider due to my age, I was not aware of it. No one made any overt negative remarks, such as, "Why are *you* here?"

I told my wife after the first week of school that I was now a "bro," because that was an ever-present term of exchange among the students at UTI: *"Hey, Bro—", "I wouldn't do that, Bro", "Where you going for lunch, Bro?"* Clearly, this school was steeped in "bro" culture. I never heard anyone at UTI refer to another student as "dude." My wife and I both chuckled about my new label, but I was secretly pleased. By calling me "bro," the other students were including me in their world.

A number of my fellow students in Basic Engines would become my closest friends during my year at UTI. Although the entire class was purposefully split up after Basic Engines (as some students were enrolled in various other programs in addition to Automotive Technology and thus had other courses they were required to take), a large number of us continued through another five courses together. After that, I saw at least one or two of my former Basic Engines classmates in almost all my courses. The bonding experience of Basic Engines creates a lot of camaraderie among the students. However, there was also a passion for cars and trucks that we all shared. Everyone joined in any discussion regarding cars and trucks, and shared stories about driving. There were lively debates on which cars or trucks were better than others, the challenges of working on certain cars, where to buy the best tools, Ford vs. Chevy, foreign vs. domestic, and Jeep vs. everyone else. My friend group was markedly enthusiastic about being in school to learn more about working on various cars and trucks. I am convinced that this passion will make these guys successful technicians.

Another distinct memory I have from my first week at UTI is that the other students were unfailingly polite, not only to me, but also to each other. It could be that everyone was trying to be on their best behavior. It could have been that they saw I was older and thus tried to act more "grown up" in front of me. But at 6:00 AM, when you are shuffling into school in order to be ready for class and you are tired and lugging a heavy backpack (or just yourself) into the building before the sun rises, and you instinctively hold the door for the next person or group coming through—that is nothing less than *polite*. Students holding the door for others was just one example of the politeness I consistently observed at UTI but was not initially expecting to see. I also heard plenty of "please" and "thank you" on campus. Perhaps it was just a "first week" phenomenon. Perhaps this politeness was restricted to certain people I just happened to notice. I admit, I was pleasantly surprised. I was somewhat apprehensive when I first enrolled at UTI of being a "fish out of water" in my new technical school environment. I wasn't sure if the other students would be "rough around the edges" or bullies, have anger management issues, or simply be bitter, feeling they were forced to attend because no other options were available to them. To underscore my initial apprehension, some of the other students were physically larger than I am. I was therefore duly impressed with how nice people were to each other that first week of school.

I already mentioned Correda, the victim of my "off script" introduction the first day of class, and Rogers, the guy who earned SOC in my Basic Engines course. Rogers owns two Jeeps, which he dearly loves. He was the "Jeep" voice during our various car discussions. He lived in off-campus housing along with another Basic Engines friend, Gordon. Gordon had amassed a considerable amount of experience with cars even though he had only recently graduated from high school. He hung around with other "car guys" in his hometown and had regularly bought and sold cars during high school. He once shared that he had bought and sold eleven different cars, many of them worth only a few hundred dollars, by the time he graduated high school. He divulged that he had been called down to the principal's office on his high school graduation day because he had done a huge burnout in front of the school that morning at the encouragement of some of his friends. He also admitted that his parents were not pleased with his driving antics. At one point, his parents installed a tracking device in his car. Gordon soon figured out how he could defeat this device. He would drive his car to his friend's house, turn off the car, disconnect the battery, remove the tracking device from the car, put the car battery back in the car, and then drive all night with his friends without the tracking device recording his whereabouts. At the end of the evening, he reversed the process so the tracking device would show only that he spent the entire night at his friend's house. I could not believe what I was hearing! As a concerned parent, I was horrified. As an aspiring auto tech, I thought, *Way to go!*

There was Westbrook, who was in his late twenties. He was married with two small children. His wife worked, so if the babysitter did not show up, he had to stay home to take care of the kids, which would cause him to miss class from time to time. He was a funny guy who had a coveted job as a tech in a Toyota dealership. Given that he was a little older, many of the other students looked to him for guidance on working, relationships, and dating girls—which he willingly shared.

There was Baker, who loves Chevy trucks and country music. At the time, he drove an older Silverado that was "lifted" off the ground. Baker was entertaining. He loved to yell out, "Hell yeah!" in class whenever any instructor mentioned Chevys or trucks.

There was Valdez, the butt of Mr. M's joke, who had moved to the US just a few years earlier. He worked in a warehouse but was really committed to training as an auto technician so he could make more money and climb the ladder of success. Valdez was an earnest guy who tried very hard to keep up with the rest of us. In Basic Engines, he expressed his dream of getting high enough grades to be hired by Porsche or BMW into their elite training programs. Over the course of the school year, however, he was unable to maintain the elevated grade point average required to be in the running for those positions. That limitation did not dampen his dreams, though. Countless times, Valdez declared he was looking forward to graduating from UTI, landing a high-paying job, and living large. He once mused, "Once I get a tech job, I'm going to move out of the house (he lived at home with his parents), buy myself some new clothes, and have enough money to take a girl out on a date." He was dreaming big, and I admired him for that.

And there was Temple, who hailed from a small town and had extensive experience working on German cars. He was generous with his knowledge, and I often sought his advice on how to do an oil change on my Audi, how to change the wheels, where to find the best deals on Audi parts, and so forth. Temple is short in stature, which made him stand out from most of the other students at UTI. He was also at the same new student orientation session I attended. I passed him going into the men's room that morning, and he was so small and so young-looking that I thought he must be another student's little brother, not a student himself.

Temple had a great sense of humor and liked to make jokes when he could. I was the butt of his jokes once. He declared, "You know, Ellis, when I saw you for the first time during orientation, I said to myself, 'What is *that* guy doing here?'" The other students snickered at this "dig" but I just smiled.

Once the laughter died down, I retorted, "You know, Temple, when I saw *you* during orientation, I thought the same thing." *Mic drop.* The guys fell on the ground laughing, and Temple knew I could give as good as I got. One of the few times in my life when I had the bigger laugh.

One of my lab partners in Basic Engines was Alonzo. Alonzo was street smart and also possessed a great deal of practical auto tech experience. He was my reference during Basic Engines for determining how best to tackle the labs, particularly anything involving the tear-down or rebuilding of the engine. I sat next to Alonzo in several other courses during my year, and we were always lab partners because we both wanted to do the labs correctly and attain high lab scores. Alonzo and I were students in the same Advanced Diagnostics course during the year, around January or February. One morning in that class, Alonzo mentioned he'd had a flat tire on his way to school. There was a snowstorm that day, but notwithstanding the inclement weather, he was able to remove the flat tire with the tools he kept in his trunk, put on the spare tire, stop at a gas station to fill the spare tire with more air, and arrive at school before the first bell rang. And he even documented his efforts that morning on video, using his smartphone. He showed me the footage before class began. *I could never have done that!*

These were only a handful of the students I met in Basic Engines, but they are representative of the students I met during the year in my various courses. They accepted me as a fellow student, for which I am grateful. They made me feel like just "one of the guys."

I managed to keep my exact age a secret until my second course when I was "outed" by the instructor, Mr. V. "Who here does not yet have a job?" asked Mr. V during the first week of the course Automotive Power Trains (aka Manual Transmissions). Mr. V is an energetic instructor and is exceptionally enthusiastic about everything. He also teaches in the Ford program at school, which is a student-paid additional program focusing exclusively on Ford cars. He encouraged all of us to get jobs while we were in school in order to obtain some practical experience. Since I am retired and had no interest in working while I was attending school, I made the fatal mistake of raising my hand. Everyone in that course heard me spill the beans: I had no job, was retired, was a former lawyer, and was sixty-two. Despite my secret being out, no one made a big deal about it. I was occasionally teased about my age by my friends (usually with reference to my balding head), but nothing that I found offensive. My age was probably irrelevant to most of the other students. Their minds and interests were focused on other things, and I'm grateful that no one tried to pick on me because of my age. Other students who did not know me sometimes asked me how old I was. My response was always the same: "I'm younger than I look" or "I'm really old. Let's just leave it at that." That usually curtailed any conversations about my age.

My prior life as a lawyer did not seem to draw much attention either. At age eighteen or nineteen, the other students probably did not know many lawyers. I think for most of them, a lawyer is someone they see on television, not someone they have met personally. So, their view of lawyers is limited to what they see on screen or from what their friends tell them. Their image of a lawyer is likely limited to a stereotypical criminal lawyer or a family lawyer (if their parents were divorced) or maybe even an attorney who represents defendants in traffic court. When I explained what I did as a lawyer, which involved multinational corporations and tax planning, their eyes immediately glazed over from the very first word I uttered ("multinational"). It really did not matter to them what I did. Their sense was that I was different from them, but it was of no real consequence. I tried not to make my prior career sound really interesting to them. Even if I wanted to do that, any such effort on my part would be doomed to failure. What eighteen- or nineteen-year-old really wants to hear what a lawyer does?

I never asked people whether they knew anything about me. However, given that students *do* gossip and talk about other students all the time, I suspect that some people heard through the grapevine that I used to be a lawyer. One student I had never met before did in fact approach me in one class. He asked me if it was true that I was once a lawyer.

I responded, "Yes."

He then gave me a perplexed look, and asked, "You must have been a crooked lawyer. Yes?" *I am not making this up.*

I think what he was trying to ask was whether I had been disbarred for being a crooked lawyer, forcing me to go back to school to learn a different profession. I assured him I was not a crooked lawyer and that I had chosen to come to school to learn. *Just to learn.* This was my refrain to everyone's inquiries about my enrollment at UTI. "I'm here to learn. That is why I'm here."

Although the other students did not seem to care much about my age, I was probably more attuned to our age differences than they were. The words of the Steely Dan song, "Hey Nineteen" come immediately to mind:

No we got nothing in common
No we can't talk at all
Please take me along
When you slide on down[15]

I felt like a *stranger in a strange land* due to our age differences, but the other students ignored that fact and, in my presence, they talked amongst themselves the same as if I was their age. I felt privileged, in a way, to be included in their conversations. They were eighteen or nineteen, and they acted like people of that age. They were, for the most part, full of energy and very restless. They were constantly on their phones: scrolling through photos and videos, texting their friends, playing video games. Most of them hated school and wanted to finish as soon as possible so they could go out into the world and make money. I had also forgotten that students their age ate *tons* of junk food. Vending machines at the school had to be replenished daily with chips, candy, cupcakes, and sweet rolls to meet the relentless demand. The drink choices at UTI were largely relegated to soft drinks. Only two machines in the building sold cups of coffee and the coffee was terrible! I rarely saw any other students drink coffee. I was surrounded constantly by snack food, junk food, energy drinks, pop, and—whenever students could leave campus to pick up lunch—fast food. The grand prize of all food groups was reserved for *pizza.* *Everyone* wanted pizza, and they ate it during both breakfast and

---

15   © 1980 Music and Lyrics by Walter Becker and Donald Fagen.

lunch breaks. Whenever the school put on a special presentation or on days that allowed for an extensive lunch period, tons of pizzas were ordered. And when UTI hosted special lunches honoring students who won awards, what did they serve? You guessed it: *pizza*. It was definitely not my food of choice.

As a "Bro", I was privy to an assortment of conversations among other students during breaks, in the hallways, or even before the start of each school day. As kids fresh out of high school, the bulk of their conversations—when not about money or their "fucking jobs"—were about girls and sex. There were plenty of stories of meeting girls on Tinder, bad dates, wild parties with lots of sex (some of which probably never actually transpired), and strategies for "picking up" girls. More than once, Westbrook offered the other guys sage advice in this regard. "Guys, you can't just go up to a girl you see on the street and ask her out," he would advise. "You have to say hello to her. Compliment her on something like her hair, what she is wearing, or talk about something she is interested in. Do that first before you ask her out." He was the voice of experience, and the other guys knew it. I refrained from joining in this topic of conversation. I don't have a lot of "pick up" experience, and whatever experience I do have is probably too antiquated to be of any real help.

During one break in our Manual Transmissions course, about ten people held an informal debate on dating: where to find the best-looking girls, what kinds of girls they prefer, what makes a girl "hot," etc. Many aspects of the discussion were clearly sexist, misogynistic, and certainly a reflection of their age. *These are just kids,* I remember thinking at the time. One student declared that he exclusively dated older women, and by "older women," he meant "grandmas." The group collectively ribbed him for that one, but he insisted that the sex was better with a more experienced woman. He mentioned he was dating an older woman who gave him money from time to time. "She's my *sugar momma*," he said. The group also discussed whether they ever dated any black girls, whether they preferred white girls over black girls, and vice versa. I could not believe I was listening to this, and almost walked out of the room, troubled by the trajectory of the discussion. But the group was a mix of Caucasian, African-American, and Latino guys, and the tenor of their discussion was earnest and matter-of-fact, so it did not seem like anyone was being antagonistic towards one another. They were pretty open about their preferences. The matter of preferences concluded, they moved on to swapping strategies on how to meet girls on the street and what were the best pick-up lines. No one could agree on what line works the best. What they all could agree on, however, was where to go to meet the best-looking girls. The hands-down favorite pick-up spot: Kmart. Not Target or Walmart. *Kmart.* I went home and told my wife about this discussion, and the two of us could not stop laughing about the specificity and novelty of Kmart as a singles hot spot. But to these students, it was their reality and it's what they believed.

Since most of the students at school were testosterone-charged young men, it was not surprising that any female in the building received a lot of attention. One day our instructor interrupted his lecture as a group of people passed by the door to the classroom and said, "Since everyone is looking out into the hallway instead of staring at the board, I can only assume that females must be walking by." *Sure enough*, several young women, clearly part of a tour group visible in the hallway, passed by as he uttered those words. Heads always seemed to turn towards the door and hallway whenever a female walked by.

As is probably typical with high school–age kids, I witnessed the endless teasing of certain students for a variety of reasons. The targeted students stood out from the rest in some way. They were always late or they looked different or they said or did something offbeat in class. A few students earned nicknames: "Corn Chips" (because he was always eating snack chips in class), "Peanut Butter" (not sure where that one came from), and "Master Tech" (because he claimed he knew more than the other students). I never heard anyone call me a nickname, but that does not mean I did not have one.

Pranks were commonplace on campus. One popular prank entailed stealing someone's ID badge and hiding it, either by putting it on the instructor's desk or by clipping it to the pull cord for the window blinds. Other pranks included moving someone's binder to a different place in the room, taking someone's coat and wearing it, or even writing something about the person on the whiteboard. Some students couldn't resist the temptation to draw funny pictures on the whiteboard when the instructor was out of the classroom. Horseplay was also prevalent. Some students playfully punched their friends hard in the arm or tapped them on the shoulder, then pretended they had not done anything when their friends turned around to investigate. Some students liked to roughhouse and chase each other if the instructor was not paying attention. During the lunch break in one particular course, I recall, two students wrestled each other to the ground in a playful "King of the Mountain" show of strength. This wrestling match continued every lunch period for an entire week. I have no idea what the backstory was with *that* one. They were always smiling and laughing while wrestling with each other. The other students ignored their playfulness, and so did I.

For amusement, and when the instructor was congenial enough to accept it, some students would make funny noises during class. Again, I view this behavior as reflective of the age of the students and not of the school itself. The most common crowd-pleasers were fart noises. I caught myself laughing sometimes—not at the fart noises but because everyone else was also laughing. Laughter is contagious, even if it is for a juvenile prank like a fake fart. You remember Correda from Basic Engines, the student I introduced as being able to kick everyone's ass? Well, he was a jokester himself, as it turns out. He came out of his shell by the third course. I don't know its source, but to make everyone in class laugh he sometimes—*unprovoked*—yelled out, "Can I get a 'HY-YUH?'" To which the class would respond, "HY-YUH!" I'm not sure what it means (perhaps the origins stem from his tae kwon do class), and the few people I asked could not explain its provenance. But it seemed to catch on and people enjoyed the call-and-response. He would yell it out before class started, as we waited for the bell at the end of class, during breaks, in the hallway—basically whenever he was moved to call it out. Correda was rather proud of his invention. One time he told me he had been waiting in line in the men's room to use the urinal when out of the blue he yelled out, "Can I get a 'HY-YUH?'" To his amusement, and everyone else's in the bathroom, everyone sitting on the throne behind their closed doors responded in unison, "HY-YUH!" Juvenile? Perhaps, but it was a way these young men had fun and blew off steam at school.

Despite my initial assumption, age was NOT the big differentiator between me and the other students. The difference was *money*. I was financially comfortable and almost all of the other students were not. At the beginning of school, I was not aware of how financially strapped many of the students who sat next to me in class were. I think it's safe to characterize most of them as living "hand to mouth." Tuition at UTI is expensive. My one year of education cost me $35,000, and I could afford to pay it. Those students who signed up for additional courses, such as manufacture-specific training, or those who failed a course and had to retake it, had even heftier tuition bills. For the most part, these students did not come from wealthy families. They came from working families where every member of employment age had a job. Some of the students at UTI lived at home or shared apartments with other students in order to make ends meet. Almost every student had a full-time or part-time job in addition to attending six hours of school every weekday. These jobs were often entry level and did not pay a lot of money. The students might earn $12 or $14 per hour as lube techs doing oil changes and tire rotations at local dealerships, but at that hourly rate, they did not make much, especially if the jobs were part-time only.

Almost all of these students accumulate substantial loans or rely on financial aid. All of them have to drive to school and then to their jobs once class lets out, so the cost of gas and maintenance of their cars constitutes a large part of their budget. One of my friends confided in me that he had to cut back on what he was eating every day because he could not afford to buy both groceries for the week and gas for his car. The car won out. He was a big guy during Basic Engines but by the time he shared his predicament with me several courses later, he had already lost twenty pounds. UTI provides a food pantry in its Student Services department so students who are desperate can get basics, such as cans of tuna fish or ramen noodles, to tide them over until payday. The necessity of the food pantry is just a reflection of the economic challenges that most UTI students face while they are attending classes. One illuminating example of these economic hardships arose during UTI's open house, when I first enrolled. One of the UTI speakers emphasized how the employment department works hard to find jobs for every student who attends the school, both during school and after graduation. He described a number of jobs that local businesses and merchants make available to UTI students. He referred to them as "survivor jobs" due to their low pay. It was not until I got to school that I fully understood how the UTI students really struggle to make ends meet with these "survivor jobs." Many students came to school in worn work shoes and boots, very thin coats or no coats (even in the frigid winter months), and often resorted to putting their arms inside their T-shirts to stay warm in class. And absolutely no one had an umbrella. I think I was the only one who brought an umbrella to school whenever it rained.

Money for UTI students is always tight. They freely admit their poverty to their fellow students and share stories of how they struggle to make ends meet. They are not trying to outdo each other, like the *Monty Python* routine that includes the dialogue:

"When I grew up, my family lived in a paper bag."

"Oh, in my family, we always *dreamed* of living in a paper bag."[16]

The students were very matter-of-fact about their circumstances. I was surprised about their candor, but they were also very resilient. My sensitivity to the poverty that the majority of students experience made me very circumspect whenever the subject of money arose. I also felt it inappropriate for me to talk about my home, the neighborhood where I live, my cars, my legal career, my college and law school education—or even my upbringing. I was acutely aware of the economic divide that existed between me and many of the other students, and I didn't want to talk about it. I did not want them to think I was somehow bragging about my successes and fortune when so many of them had very little and were just starting out in their careers. I jealously guarded my status as "one of the guys" or "just another student." Those students who knew me or who heard me spill the beans in Manual Trans about my prior career understood I had been a lawyer and that I was different, but I did not want to make a show of it or be labelled a show-off. So, I did not talk about myself at all.

As an example of how the scarcity of money impacts UTI students, a friend of mine once told me he was worried about his GPA because he was missing so many days of school. He said his car had broken down, and he had to cut classes every now and then so he could earn extra money at his job to pay for his car repairs. He had no other way to get to school and had no support system if his car broke down. He could not ride along to school with another student since he lived far away from everyone else. He did not have family who could lend him a car or drive him to and from school and his

---

16 "Four Yorkshiremen," Brooke-Taylor, Cleese, Chapman, and Feldman (1967).

job. He could not just call an Uber or Lyft to drive him to school because the expense would be far too great. His was a day-to-day existence. Lack of money had a significant impact on students' success. Its absence meant that some students could not even attend classes consistently—something for which they were paying dearly for with tuition, thus affecting their grades and their learning.

My desire to keep my prior life a secret meant that I was in a significant way "undercover." I was reminded of the show *Undercover Boss*, in which the president or CEO of some company uses an alias to work at a branch or department in his company so he can see what really goes on with his employees. In this case, however, I was not anyone's "boss." I was just "undercover." As much as the conversation in class might turn to a topic about which I knew a lot, I often did not chime in because it might be misconstrued as "showing off" or bragging. Even though I really was *not* "one of the guys" in every way, I still felt like a part of the group. I loved the camaraderie and the feeling that I was part of something bigger than myself. In a way, hanging out with the other students—even as an "undercover" former lawyer—echoed the camaraderie and fun I once had while practicing law. Clearly the conversations were different but there was a lot of passion and, in many cases, a lot of funny stories.

As you might expect with teenagers who drive cars, there is a fair amount of "spirited" driving by UTI students—including driving at high speeds in the school parking lot (the posted speed limit is 5 mph, but almost no one adhered to it), zooming down the local roads leading up to school, and "doing donuts."[17] I have never understood the attraction of doing donuts, but UTI students were universally enthusiastic about doing them—especially after it rained and the ground was particularly slick. Doing donuts in the school parking

17 Spinning the rear tires so fast that the car naturally goes around in a circle, leaving circular skid marks on the pavement.

lot was strictly prohibited, and its unconditional ban was a major bullet point during SOPs. That did nothing to stem the practice, however. The school parking lot is filled with security cameras and just about everyone who did donuts in the school parking lot got caught. The penalty was not just an infraction. You immediately failed your current course. The penalty was big, to fit the crime.

UTI students' propensity for aggressive driving on public roads outside of the school property was a big concern for the administration, and we often were told to observe posted speed limits *"or else."* A local police officer visited our classroom several times during the year to remind us to obey the law. We were told that neighbors in nearby office buildings complained frequently about the noise, tire squealing, and fast driving by UTI students as they left school at the end of classes. The police officer strenuously repeated his warnings to us to adhere to the local speed laws. At one point the complaints reached a crescendo, requiring this same officer to return with a special *new* warning. He informed us that the tenants of the nearby office buildings were offices of various federal agencies (including the FBI) and that their jurisdiction extended to the roadways outside of their offices. He warned us that if we were caught speeding on the public roads in front of those offices, we would be arrested by federal agents, who would take us downtown to the federal courthouse where we would sit in a federal jail for a long time until our case was heard by a federal magistrate. The room got eerily silent when he said those words, but I did not believe a word of it. I thought it was all bullshit. I think the police officer made it up to scare the students.

By the way, the "spirited" driving continued unabated, *even after that dire warning.*

Given their stretched budgets, many UTI students cannot afford to drive nice cars. Many cars and trucks I saw in the UTI parking lot were in pretty rough shape. They are inexpensive, worth very little money, or are older and high-mileage cars. Some students, who possess the know-how and tools or who work in a dealership or independent shop, have the opportunity to repair their own cars to save some money, but that does not apply to everyone at the school. Some students have nice cars—perhaps not late model, but they run and the students keep them clean. Other cars clearly reflect the considerable work that students have put into them either because they have aftermarket wheels, the trucks are "lifted," or the cars sport custom lights or window tinting. Some students drive their *work* cars to school, such as one student who parked a taxi in the parking lot every day. On the day of his graduation, an entire fleet of the same type of taxi from the same company flooded the parking lot. I expect many of his taxi driver colleagues arrived *en masse* as a show of support for his graduation. Some of the better-looking cars were showcased by students at the student car shows that UTI hosted routinely throughout the year.

The sorry state of many students' cars is a standing joke for the instructors. As many of the less expensive cars happen to be older foreign cars, those cars are the ones many students drove to school. The instructors, as a rule, poked fun at foreign cars. The most consistent targets of their scorn were Japanese cars. Honda, Toyota, and Subaru are good, reliable cars. However, the instructors would make endless jokes about their puny four-cylinder engines, the "fart cans" that some students would add to make their cars sound more powerful (and thus make people think they were faster), and cars that students had lowered so much that they appeared to scrape the ground. My instructors, in general, favored American muscle cars and large engines. *"There is no replacement for displacement"* was their mantra, meaning that cars with large engines (e.g., engines with eight cylinders, unlike most foreign cars that have only four cylinders) are superior to any cars with smaller engines. The instructors' jokes were good-natured, but I suspect those students with shitty cars did not keep their cars in that state on purpose. They just could not afford anything better.

Which brings me to my car. I do *not* have a shitty car. The car I drove to UTI on a daily basis is a 2014 Audi S4. Audi is the luxury division of Volkswagen. I did not drive my Audi to school to show off, but it is the least ostentatious car I own. It has a V-6 supercharged engine, 333 horsepower, and a leather interior, and is incredibly nimble and rock solid on the road. I keep it in good condition and wash and wax it frequently.

Before I started my program at UTI, I wondered if it was wise for me to drive this car to school. My primary fear was vandalism. One of my other cars was keyed (when someone purposely scratches the paint on the car with a key or other metal object) a few years before when it was parked at the local hospital while I visited my mom, who was undergoing treatment there. I was understandably distressed when I found my car in that condition, and it took two re-sprays of the car (which took several months) to fix all of the damage. The vandal or vandals had keyed both sides of the car, meaning many different body panels on the car had to be repainted. As a result, I was leery about the possibility that my Audi S4 might get vandalized in the UTI parking lot. I was hesitant about leaving my car parked in an open lot all day while I was in class. I mentioned my vandalism concerns at lunch one day while I was still working at the law firm. One of my partners suggested I buy a "beater car" and drive it to school every day. That suggestion made sense superficially, but in a way it really *didn't* make sense. Why would I try to pretend that my beater car was really my car? And what if someone found out that I was just trying to make it look like I did not have a nice car? I would be mortified. However, another partner who lives in a town near the school calmed my fears. "I am pretty sure they won't harm your car," he assured me. "We really don't see that type of thing in our neck of the woods." In the end I did not purchase a beater car to drive to UTI.

Understandably, the S4 immediately got a lot of attention at school. As a sporty car it became a topic of conversation, and the other students coveted it. I no longer had to worry about vandalism. The other students in Basic Engines soon found out it was my car. They asked me a lot of questions, such as: "How much horsepower does it have? How fast have you driven it? What is the 0–60 time? How much did it cost?" I didn't mind the questions about the car's performance, since we talked about cars all the time in class. But a question about the cost of the car was a "fishing expedition" to me and could lead to additional disclosures about how much money I made as a lawyer. I was not going down that path. My response to the question about the car's cost was always, "I don't remember."

One time, a student I did not know stopped me in the hallway during break and asked, "Is that your car, the blue Audi, in the parking lot?"

"Yes," I said.

"Sweet ride," he complimented, then continued casually down the hall.

And yes, it *is* a sweet ride. Any student who knew the car I drove to school every day likely knew I had spent a lot of money on the car and that I had more money than they did. So, despite my efforts to keep my wealth a secret, and blend in as "just one of the guys," it was undone every morning I entered the school parking lot in the Audi. My car gave me away. *Perhaps I should have gotten that beater after all . . . .*

CHAPTER 4

DO IT AGAIN

Attending a technical school like UTI is a daunting prospect for someone who has been practicing law as long as I have. It requires a radical shift in mindset: from lawyer to student, from senior partner to novice. I used to lead teams of people on international projects. At UTI I led no one and was just another guy trying to make it through the Automotive Technology program. As a senior lawyer I was a subject matter expert sought out by clients around the world for my expertise. At UTI I started at the bottom. I was learning about automotive technology from the ground up, and no one was asking me to fix their cars. At least not yet.

But perhaps the biggest challenge in making the switch from law practice to technical school was going from an unstructured, unpredictable routine as a lawyer—where I could to some extent do what I wanted or could at least influence what I did during the day—to a very repetitive, almost mechanical routine at UTI, where everything was scripted for me. After you have practiced law for a number of years, you in a significant way become master of your own universe. Certainly, there is often chaos—or at least controlled chaos—throughout each day, with multiple projects for various clients all due at the same time. Interruptions thread your day (whether in person, by phone/email, or by the sudden publication of a change in the law, requiring you to alert clients as to what the new law means for them). There is no clearly defined beginning or end of the workday. I continued to work on documents or negotiate transactions long into the night whenever necessary. But I also had the flexibility to drop everything and catch a flight to attend a client meeting or pitch to a prospective client. My phone and laptop lent me the freedom to take my office on the road at any time. I learned how to be a road warrior. I made myself available to clients at any time of the day or night, and thanks to nearly reliable airplane Wi-Fi connections, I could easily remain "on the grid," even when in flight.

At UTI, in contrast, routine is inescapable. The routine is the same, day after day after day. Classes consistently start at established times (either 6:30 AM or 6:40 AM for me, depending on which course I was taking). Bells go off five minutes prior to class and again exactly at the start of class. There is always a morning break (fifteen minutes) and a lunch break (thirty minutes). All courses that begin at 6:30 AM end by 12:45 PM with a bell, and courses that start at 6:40 AM end by 12:55 PM with another bell. Once classes are over, everyone leaves the campus except for a few hardy souls who brave an afternoon course load as well. This extended schedule is called "double coursing." Very few people do it because it leaves no time for a job outside of school. However, students who double course finish school that much faster than other students. My friend, Rogers, was one who double-coursed at UTI. He enrolled in both the Automotive Technology and the Diesel programs. We both finished at the same time and graduated together although he ended up taking more courses than I did.

Every course is exactly three weeks long. Classes are Monday through Friday, with none offered on Saturday or Sunday. One instructor is assigned to each three-week course. The first day of each course is devoted to SOPs. With a few exceptions, the last Thursday of the course is reserved for the lab final and the last Friday of the course is dedicated to the 20-point final exam. While the subject matter of each course dictates whether there are greater or fewer lab days, the class schedule is the same from course to course. The school takes one week off around Christmas and individual days off for observed holidays throughout the school year. The only other hiccup in the Monday through Friday routine may be for "snow days" or special instructor training. But in order for a student to complete the program as quickly as possible, the most expedient process is to plow through all seventeen courses, one after another, in fifty-one weeks. Accordingly, the Automotive Technology program takes an entire year to complete.

The routine for taking a 10-point multiple-choice test is identical for every course. First, you must remove everything from your desk, including your cell phone. The only item left on your desk should be a pencil with No. 2 lead. Second, the instructor distributes the blank answer sheet on which you fill out your name, the course title and number, and the instructor's name. Third, the instructor circulates individual copies of the test, which usually consists of ten multiple-choice questions. There are two versions of the test (A and B), which are distributed so that no two people sitting next to each other have the same version of the test. Both versions contain exactly the same questions, but each version lists the questions in a different order so that your table partner cannot cheat by simply glancing at your answers. You answer the questions by filling in bubbles on an answer sheet that is scanned by a machine to determine if your answers are right or wrong. Except for questions that ask if a statement is true or false, there are four possible answers for each question (A through D). Talking is banned during tests and no one is permitted to leave the room, even to go to the bathroom. Particularly strict instructors forbid anyone from leaving the room until all tests are completed, collected, and then reviewed by the instructor with the entire class.

Unbelievably, there is an unlimited amount of time to take the 10-point test. If you complete your test early, you must wait until the last person finishes his or her test before you can relax, talk to your neighbor, or even leave the room. During many tests, several of us waited for what seemed like an eternity for the last student to turn in his test. I was never the first person to finish a test—especially if I was struggling with an answer—but I was never the last one to turn in my test either. My friend Rogers was often the last person done—but he almost always got a perfect 10 on his tests, so I don't begrudge him the extra time. He was just being careful. I myself tried to be careful. I navigated each question slowly and deliberately and reviewed my work at least *three* times before I considered it completed. Despite my extra-careful approach, I still made some mistakes.

While you are waiting for everyone to finish their tests, there is an understandable urge to ask another student how he or she answered a particular question. Most instructors insist on absolute silence until all of the tests have been collected. Notwithstanding, I overhead plenty of whispering, such as "What did you put for the last question?" On one occasion, I turned my test in early and noticed my table partner was hunched over his test, still working through the questions. When the instructor looked the other way, my table partner hastily tapped my arm and gestured towards the troubling question on his test. He wanted me to give him the answer. I was both surprised and horrified that he would ask me to help him cheat. Stunned, I decided the best thing I could do was just look away. I sat there silently, contemplating the opposite wall so no one could claim I was looking at his test. He did not tap me again. After the tests were collected, he turned to me and asked me what I had put down for a particular question. I told him and he grimaced. It turned out he had guessed wrong.

Once everyone is done and the tests are collected, the instructor reviews each question with the class and shares the correct answer. Sometimes he provides the class with an explanation as to why the right answer is the right answer. These post-test reviews are informal, and the instructor usually allows students to ask for a more detailed explanation. Several times I took advantage of this opportunity, particularly if the correct answer still perplexed me. I discovered as I went along in the program that when I missed a question, it was often considered an "easy" question by the rest of the class. The "hard" questions were the ones I almost always got right. I am not sure why I missed so many "easy" questions. Perhaps it was my lack of basic knowledge, or my years of practice as a lawyer, but it could also be that I tend to overthink things. I often read too much into a question or interpret an easy question as a trick question. So, it was a common occurrence that when the instructor would give the answer to a "hard" question, there would be a lot of groans in the class from those who missed the question, but I knew I had filled in the right answer. At the same time, I can recall several times when the instructor gave the answer to an "easy" question. The class affirmed it was an easy question with a few comments of "yes" or "that was easy." I demurred, wondering to myself, *How the hell did I miss that one?* That was the test-taking routine at UTI.

I knew going in that school would be a significant change for me, and I looked forward to the new routine of being tied to a strict schedule. I fell into the rhythm of my new routine pretty quickly and had no difficulty adjusting to the change. I found it liberating no longer to be the decision maker for how to manage my time. I also enjoyed not being tied to capricious deadlines mandated by clients or firm administrative requirements. I am by nature a creature of habit, and my habits as a lawyer were not always aspirational. Someone might say they were unhealthy in some respects. When I practiced law, unless I had an early morning meeting, I often slept in, arriving at the office after 9:00 AM. I dined out frequently, especially with clients or at firm meetings, and I drank heavily (coffee during the day and alcohol at night). My schedule was always shifting to accommodate client meetings, business travel, and similar demands on my time. I almost never went to bed at the same time at night, and I did not wake up at the same time each day. I was constantly glued to my cell phone, checking my messages, responding to colleagues or clients, reviewing my flight schedule or the weather, or catching up on the news. I stayed up very late every night to finish any outstanding work. I liked to say that I did my best work after 10:00 pm. Because I lived so close to work, I went into the office every day, even on weekends. In short, I was a workaholic.

As a UTI student, I quickly broke those old habits and routines. I woke up at 4:15 AM *every morning* to make it to class on time. I drove the same route to school every day—which may have been born of necessity more than routine, as it was the only route from my house. I originally tried waking up at 4:30 AM and leaving the house at 5:30 AM, figuring an hour would be enough time for me to make what Waze™[18] indicated was a 35-minute commute. This schedule worked fine until the first day of my Basic Electronics class, when I arrived late (not a way to make a good first impression on the instructor). A traffic accident had blocked all lanes on the highway leading to the school. Mortified that I was late (which, by the way, is a "tension dream" I often have when I am under stress), I made sure to wake up no later than 4:15 AM and be in my car by 5:00 AM from then on. I was never late to school after that. The extra time buffer allowed me to stop in the Dunkin Donuts near the campus and pick up decent coffee before heading over to school. I often had time to spare to sit in my car in the school parking lot and read the *New York Times* and other news apps on my phone before the building opened at 6:00 AM.

I parked in the exact same spot in the UTI parking lot every day. I considered it "my" spot and was annoyed if someone else got

---

18   Waze is a GPS navigation software application owned by Google, which works on GPS-enabled tablets and smartphones (*Wikipedia*, n.d.).

there before me and took my coveted space away from me. From that vantage point, I could see, through my windshield, the corner of the school building and the entrance lobby. I could also see the security badge reader on the side of the building. It remained "red" until 6:00 AM, meaning you needed an approved badge to swipe the reader and unlock the door. At 6:00 AM every day, the security badge reader turned "green," automatically unlocking the doors to the building. At that point, anyone could just open the door and walk in.

As I often arrived in the parking lot early, around 5:45 AM, I observed most other students pull in their cars after me. Like me, these students had their preferred parking spots. I knew some of them from the various courses I had taken, but we rarely talked or even made eye contact during the few minutes before the doors opened. I think everyone in that parking lot just wanted some "alone" or "me" time before the beginning of school, so I did not try to engage with anyone. Every morning I saw Mr. M (the instructor from Basic Engines) enter the building at 5:50 AM. Thus, a new morning ritual began for me: sitting in the parking lot, drinking my Dunkin Donuts coffee, reading the news on my phone, and waiting for Mr. M to swipe his badge and enter the building. A few other instructors would also sometimes enter the building through this entrance. Occasionally, I noticed a hapless student try to enter the building before 6:00 AM, when the security badge reader was still "red." He or she would invariably pull on the doors a few times, peer through the glass to see if anyone was inside who could open the door, and then just hang out by the entrance until the doors magically unlocked, permitting entrance into the building.

Because I was now spending so much time in my car, I modified my car radio listening habits. I had often tuned in to rock music for the short drive to my office when I was a lawyer. I tried that approach for a few weeks as a UTI student, but the incessant commercials started to annoy me over the long drive. As I grew up in a house where classical music was always playing on the radio, I decided to switch to classical music for my drive. You know what? Classical music had an immediate calming effect, regardless of any chaos outside as I drove the highway at 5:00 AM. I felt relaxed and less stressed about the morning commute, traffic, or any pesky test or lab tests I had to face that day. On the way home from school, I alternated my accompaniment between classical music and the National Public Radio (NPR) station. I found that listening to NPR kept me informed on local, national, and world news. Up to that point, my wife had been the undisputed authority in our house as to world events because she spends so much time reading the newspaper during her commute to work and listening to news radio as she exercises every morning. I used my time driving to and from school to catch up to her. I really enjoyed becoming more aware of current events in this manner, which was something I'd had little time to do as a lawyer. I also managed to slip in some enlightening and entertaining podcasts, including the much beloved *Car Talk*.

I turned off my cell phone every day before class and did not turn it back on, except to check messages during our two mandated breaks. Detaching myself from my cell phone was hard, *very hard*, since it was my "lifeline" when I was a lawyer. But as a retired lawyer I quickly discovered that no one was emailing or texting me anymore, so I overcame that reflex quickly. After class I would head home and spend the afternoon and early evening reviewing the course materials and studying. I finished dinner by 7:30 PM and was in bed by 9:15 PM. On most nights I got a good seven hours of sleep. I arose early and went to bed early on weekends too, even though I had no class on weekends, so my body would not slip back into my old "night owl" pattern.

I purposely became a bookworm. I wanted to learn as much as I possibly could about cars, and I did not want any distractions from my goal. For this reason, I did not seek out a part-time job, as many

other UTI students did. I certainly did not need the money, and I
felt I could better spend my time reading and studying. Frankly, I was
not keen about the prospect of going to an interview and explaining
why a retired lawyer was embarking on a new career. In hindsight, I
probably would have gained some valuable hands-on experience if
I had taken a job—and I probably would still have been successful
in school. But I was not willing to risk it. Getting through school
was my sole focus for the year. I figured that I could pick up valuable
working experience once I was finally done with school.

My study routine was the same every day: I would sit down at the
dining room table, spread out my binder, my course materials, and
my Course Book, and review the morning lesson. Everything was
new to me—I mean *everything*. This was the first time I was exposed
to the underlying mechanisms in automobiles, and everything was
so novel that I wanted to ensure I understood all of the material.
If I did not understand something, and the course materials were
no more illuminating, I often searched online for other sources of
information. I also purchased several e-books on a variety of topics
(e.g., transmissions, electronics, suspensions) that were helpful. Some
of the automotive systems required a working knowledge of electronic circuit theory. For example, in our Basic Electronics course,
we needed to understand electron flow. The conventional approach is
that excess electrons flow from positive to negative; that is, they flow
out of the positive terminal of a battery into the negative terminal. In
actuality, excess electrons flow from negative to positive. That is the
Electron Theory approach. To avoid confusion, auto manufacturers
have adopted the conventional school of thought and all instruction
and repair manuals are written from this perspective. The battery's
positive terminal is really the negative terminal but has been labelled
as the positive terminal so that everyone who understands the conventional approach thinks that the positive terminal is where the

electrons are originating. *Confused?* I certainly was, so I had to look up a few additional resources before I had a firm grasp of the concept.

After a few weeks, I found that listening to some background music relaxed me while I was studying, provided the music did not distract me. I am sure I asked Alexa™ to play music from any number of different music genres and artists before I found the perfect study companion: Steely Dan. I have always liked Steely Dan. I know the lyrics to many of their songs, and the music takes me back to the time when I was a high school student, a college student, and a law student. It was the theme music of those years. I never did go to one of their concerts, which I understand are popular with a lot of men of my generation (known as "Steely Dads"). I don't have a Steely Dan T-shirt, either. But I have found that listening to a great song from back in the day has an almost mystical ability to transport you back to that period of your life. I can't explain it. Listening to Steely Dan must have triggered some joy and satisfaction in my brain as I studied for my UTI tests. And thus, Steely Dan music became a permanent fixture of my normal study routine. My wife might have wondered why she came home from work to the same music playing in the dining room every night while I studied, but she never asked about it.

My daily routine was a far cry from that of other UTI students. The majority of UTI students do not return home after class. Instead, they go straight to work. They begin working at 1:30 PM or 2:00 PM and continue until their shift is over. Their jobs vary from working in a dealership or independent shop to working in a store in a retail position. It seemed to me that many students worked late, even as late as 9:30 PM or 10:00 PM. Once they get home there are not many hours left for them to study, sleep, and then wake up in order to make it to school by 6:30 AM the next day. Even if they live close to school, they are crunched for time. The result is predictable: most UTI students don't have much of an opportunity to study after school and a lot of them are severely sleep-deprived. Sleep deprivation is so rampant at UTI that most instructors routinely roust people awake in class. Sleeping in class is a no-no, of course, and can earn you an infraction or worse—you may be sent home early. We were well versed in the ban against sleeping in class from our SOPs on the first day of every course. Instructors recommended that students stand up at the back of the classroom if they felt tempted to fall asleep (since you are less likely to fall asleep if you are standing up). Alternately, students were told to go get some coffee or get something to eat to avoid falling asleep. One instructor even went so far as to declare that no one was permitted to put their heads down on the desk, ever. *Yes, it's as bad as that.*

My first encounter with sleeping students was in my second course, Manual Trans. Our previous instructor, Mr. M of Basic Engines, was so engaging in his lectures, and his recounting of funny "war" stories from the auto industry was so entertaining, that students were always wide awake during his course. However, the lecture material in Manual Trans is less . . . *shall we say* . . . exciting. Other students had anticipated the tedium, but I was not prepared for what I observed in Manual Trans. Some students would come into the classroom before the bell, immediately plop down onto a chair, put their heads down on their desks, and fall asleep. In their slumber, they were blissfully unaware that the bell had gone off or that the student sign-in sheet was circulating around the room. Their neighbors would have to wake them up so they could sign in, and then they would promptly go back to sleep. Or they would fall asleep during the lecture and have to be prodded awake by the instructor. I discussed the sleeping student phenomenon in Manual Trans with one of my friends from Basic Engines (who was also in Manual Trans).[19] "Can you believe that guy in the front row, falling asleep in front of the instructor?" he asked, shocked. I could *not* believe it, actually. During one particular lecture, I noticed no fewer than seven students asleep in class. I caught the eye of one of my Basic Engines friends, and we both shook our heads and chuckled.

I am pretty sure the instructor, Mr. V, was aware of the rampant sleeping in his class. I find it hard to believe that anyone could stand in front of a class delivering a lecture and not notice the state of the room. He did send one student, Miller, home early one day. Miller sat several chairs away from me. He looked tired all the time, and he always looked like he had slept in his clothes. Miller religiously laid his head down on his desk as soon as he came into class. The instructor, Mr. V, had given him a warning earlier that particular day, but Miller simply could not help himself. When Mr. V strode over to Miller to inform him that he was sending him home for the day, it took Miller several minutes to wake up and realize where he was and that he had been dismissed for the day. The room became very quiet as Miller was escorted out of class. He came back the next day, however, and Mr. V never had to wake him up again after that. I know Miller got an infraction, but he ended up passing the course anyway.

I once heard a student ask another student in Manual Trans, "Bro, why you so tired all the time?"

---

19   You do not attend the same courses with the exact same students throughout the Automotive Technology program. After Basic Engines, UTI assigns the students to different courses depending on what particular programs the students have selected and which instructors are available to teach. A large group of us continued on to Manual Trans together, but not the entire Basic Engines class. Other students moved on to the Brakes course and others went to a different course. UTI starts a new group of students every three weeks. So, with every new course I was thrown in with a new mix of students, some of whom I knew but many of whom I did not. As a result, I was able to meet new students in every course I took at UTI.

The response: "Bro, I work until 10:00 PM every night. I can't get enough sleep."

Similarly, my friend Valdez often told me how little sleep he had gotten the night before because he had to work very late. He had a job at a warehouse. It sounded like he often covered for other employees who had not shown up for their shifts, making his workday even longer. More than once, he told me that the night before class he got off work at midnight or 1:00 AM.

I saw students asleep in almost every course I took. Some of them were recidivists, and the instructor would have to wake them up on almost a daily basis. When I first encountered sleeping students, I was highly critical of them. My initial judgment was that they were fools for wasting their tuition money by sleeping through lectures. My thinking was, *Why would you spend so much money on tuition and then not take advantage of every moment that you are in class to learn something?* Before I fully comprehended their challenging daily schedules, I assumed they were sleeping through class because they were bored by the subject matter. In truth, some lectures were a bit dry, so I could understand if someone did not want to listen to all of it. I myself occasionally stood at the back of the room during particularly monotonous lectures when I did not feel the need to take notes. And yes, there were probably a small percentage of students who really did not care very much for the lectures and felt no guilt about sleeping through class, regardless of the lecture material. Those types of students exist at every school. But there are other students who try their best but also have a grueling schedule in which getting enough sleep is simply not feasible. One student confided in me that his house is always "full of noise." He has a large family, with younger brothers and sisters, so there is always commotion: music, talking, and yelling. "It is *never* quiet in my house," he lamented. "Never. Day and night. Coming and going. I cannot even *think*, it is *so noisy*." So not all UTI students who fall asleep are foolishly frittering away their education.

For some, it's a daily struggle to attend class, put in long hours at a job after school, and study under less-than-optimal conditions—all in the hopes of carving out a life where they can make more money and perhaps get more sleep.

Another student chatted me up a few days before he was going to graduate. Donnellon, as it turns out, lived just a few miles from me and had almost the same commute to school as I did each morning. He mentioned that he lived in a three-flat owned by his aunt and that his apartment was located on the top floor. His younger brother and grandfather shared the flat with him. His grandfather was an invalid who needed a lot of assistance. Donnellon always showed up late to class (although he did pass the course), and I now know the reason for his tardiness. After he returned home from work around 9:00 PM, he had to make dinner for his younger brother and grandfather, then help bathe and take care of his grandfather. He said he rarely got enough sleep, let alone time to study for class. Hearing Donnellon's description of his own living situation made me feel spoiled. I had the luxury of coming home right after school without any obligations, chores, or responsibilities. If I was tired, I could take a nap. If I felt like studying, I could study. If I wanted to take a walk, go to the store, pick up some groceries or whatever, I had the luxury of time. *I am not like other UTI students,* I often told myself.

I would be lying if I claimed I was wide awake for every class. My very light schedule outside of school afforded me every opportunity to get done everything I needed to do in preparation for the next day and get a solid night's sleep before class. Despite my comparatively lax schedule, I sometimes found myself fighting fatigue even prior to the first break. My strategy for keeping awake was to take copious notes in every class and always ask a question if I did not fully comprehend something the instructor said. Sometimes I would "invent" a question simply to forge a break in the lecture so I could talk. It might have been a bit self-centered, but it was a successful tactic for me to stay awake.

Note-taking was also a key to my ability to learn the material. The material instructors handed out for each course included most, but not all, of the information necessary to pass the tests. Sometimes what the instructor said in the lectures—not what was on the printed page or on the PowerPoint slide—was tested as well. The instructors also provided foundational information for our lab tasks, including the lab final we were required to take at the end of each course. Several times during the initial SOPs, the instructor described in intimate detail the different tasks we would be asked to do in the lab final, giving us a helpful preview of what was coming. *I wrote that shit down, of course.*

Interestingly, I noticed that few other students took notes. Rogers took notes, and he and I often compared our written notes whenever we had to digest a complex subject. But most of the other students simply sat in class and listened. Most students also neglected to write down instructions for lab tasks. I cannot imagine how they digested the information. My guess is they did *not* digest the information, which may have been the reason so many students approached me and asked for help during labs. Often, they simply wanted me to repeat the lab instructions or explain how to perform a certain lab procedure previously covered by the instructor. It did not bother me that they asked me for help. I was always happy to share this information with other students. But I do wonder whether a little note-taking on their part could have helped them a little.

I also made sure to include in my notes anything that the instructor wrote on the board and tried to copy any drawing the instructor made so my notes would be complete. In the Electronic Diagnostics course, the instructor, Mr. M, drew a picture detailing how to connect up a DMM[20] to a car's charging system to test the output voltage of the alternator. I remember he drew it very rapidly, his hand flying across the board. I am not much of an artist myself, so I struggled to copy it accurately before he erased it and moved on to something else. Sure enough, this diagram was critical to performing correctly one of the lab assignments later in the course and also in taking a measurement during the lab final. My hastily drawn copy of what he drew on the board helped me study and prepare for both the lab assignment and the lab final. I simply had to memorize it.

I mention this one story because when Mr. M reviewed our completed lab sheets later in the course, he observed that many students got this measurement wrong because they had not hooked up the DMM correctly to the car's charging system. Mr. M's tone suddenly became very serious as he criticized the class for not taking notes. "We went over this the first day of class," he said. "I drew it on the board, and the only person who copied it down was Mr. Ellis." Everyone looked at me, and I tried not to look at anyone. I thought to myself, *Wow! This guy is good. He not only took note of me copying down his picture, he remembered my name!* By this course I was already in the habit of taking copious notes at school, so I was secretly pleased that in some small way I was doing something right. Whether any other students started taking notes as a result, I can only speculate.

It was no surprise to me that routine is so intrinsic to a technical school like UTI. Given the complexity of the material, a disciplined, almost mechanical approach to a curriculum allows men and women from a variety of backgrounds, with different skill levels and ability, to learn the basics of automotive technology. My four years of college

---

20   Digital Multi-Meter is a handheld device that tests voltage, amperage, and resistance in an electrical circuit. Each student at UTI is issued a DMM during orientation before school, and they are used often during lab tasks in many of the courses. A DMM is also an essential tool for any auto tech, so they are part of many techs' toolboxes.

and my three years of law school really did not prepare me for my one year at auto school, however. I started from square one with no real knowledge base nor experience from which I could draw. What helped me the most at UTI was my ability to listen and take notes, my willingness to raise my hand and ask a question if I did not understand something, and my reading the course material and associated background chapters in the Course Book. My legal reasoning abilities were never called upon at UTI, nor was my ability to synthesize pages and pages of legal regulations or dense statutory material. The self-study chapters in our Course Book were well written and easy to understand. Each chapter ranged in length from fifteen to forty pages and rarely did we need to read the entire chapter in one night. We were often allocated several days to work our way through a chapter.

My ability to write persuasively, or to simplify difficult legal concepts for my clients, was also not needed at UTI. With the exception of the occasional lab assignment where we had to describe the operation of a system "in our own words," I did not have the opportunity to impress the instructors with my writing skills honed from years of practicing law and communicating with clients. Instead, most of the labs required one-word answers, checking a certain box, drawing a diagram, or copying down the steps for a certain process from Mitchell's or AllData[21] (such as how to remove a part of the car's suspension or how to disarm a particular vehicle's airbag system before working on it). I understand that auto technicians do a lot of writing, so I can

---

21   Mitchell's and AllData are technical publishers that provide online information for almost all makes and models of automobiles. Technicians can research and review these websites to obtain manufacturer-specific information for the car they are working on. UTI has master subscriptions to both websites and, whenever we as students had to look up information, we often had the option of using either database for our research. Information for these technical websites is provided directly by the automobile manufacturers, and the publishers charge a subscription fee for this information. Not just schools but also shops and individuals can subscribe to these technical reference services.

appreciate the approach UTI uses to prepare students for what they will encounter in the field. But I personally hated lab assignments that involved a protracted process of copying multiple steps for a certain automotive procedure. I have arthritis in my fingers, and my right thumb (my writing hand) was fused in an operation several years ago because of joint deterioration. I cannot hold a pen or pencil very comfortably and writing for a long period of time becomes painful. Even taking notes in class was a struggle for me. As a lawyer, the limitations of my writing hand could be masked by using a laptop computer or iPad, which I did frequently for note-taking in meetings with clients. As a UTI student, however, I was not permitted to bring a laptop or iPad into class. Any writing was exclusively done using a pen or pencil—a "writing stick," as one instructor called it. One of my friends at UTI referred to the lab assignments that involved copying down extensive amounts of information as "pencil whipping."

There was no shortage of "pencil whipping" at UTI. Copying may be a trusted method for learning, since you are more likely to remember something if you write it. As I already mentioned, taking notes was a critical component of my learning process at UTI. But I think there was far too much copying of information directly from technical resources during lab assignments. I considered it "busy work" rather than a true learning opportunity. For my lab final in one of the Power & Performance courses, we had to identify ten different engine components (e.g., air intake, exhaust, etc.) that the instructor showed us in a series of slides, one slide per component. We had three minutes for each component on the screen, but for each one we had to write down three things: (1) the name of the component, (2) where the component is located in the car, and (3) the purpose or use of the component. To add to the difficulty level for me, the answer sheet was single-spaced and the lines were drawn very close together. I had to write in diminutive script to fit my answers onto the answer sheet.

My hand ached by the end of the test, but I did not complain and managed the best I could.

Every instructor presents the lectures slightly differently, as a reflection of the complexity of the material and the instructor's own teaching style. As I understand it, to promote consistency from campus to campus, the lectures are prepared by a team of people at UTI corporate headquarters. They prepare a deck of PowerPoint slides and (presumably) speaker's notes that every instructor uses for his or her course, and handout materials. In theory, then, each instructor at every UTI campus should deliver the same baseline lecture to every class. During my year at UTI, more than one instructor pointed out mistakes in the slide deck or mistakes in the written material they handed out, which they hoped would be corrected by corporate in the next version. Over my seventeen courses, the instructors identified incorrect diagrams, mislabeled pictures, or questionable wording at least half a dozen times.[22]

So, if your course schedule indicated a lecture, you knew you were going to watch a PowerPoint presentation. Often, instructors embellished the lecture with anecdotes, but some simply read the slides verbatim. Whenever a student asked a question, the lecture was always livelier. Occasionally, a PowerPoint slide would include an embedded link to a video showing how a particular component of a car worked to better illustrate the material. These videos were helpful, but some of them were very old and dated. The instructor often would distribute to the class examples of components to show us what they look like, such as transmission parts, engine thermostats, or electronic sensors. In the Climate Control course, for example, the instructor passed around various components of an air-conditioning system. In the Professional Applications course,

---

22   I, myself, noted numerous typos, misspellings, and formatting errors in the course materials handed out by the instructors, but I figured, hey this is only technical school, not law school.

we were shown various components of a car's air suspension system, airbag modules, and shock absorbers. These visual aids were extremely helpful supplements to the lecture, and for someone like me with no prior experience, they were invaluable learning tools. Suffice it to say, I saw so many things I have never seen before. Sometimes the instructor would draw on the whiteboard, which also served as the "screen" for the PowerPoint slides. In this way, the instructor could supplement the slides, underline certain key terms shown in the slide, or draw illustrative diagrams as appropriate.

Unfortunately, the PowerPoint slides were also often the reason why students fell asleep in class. The slides were primarily composed of fragment sentences and blocks of words. Occasionally, photographs of components or charts or graphics broke the visual monotony, but more often than not, the slides just showcased a chunk of text. The handouts were often almost a carbon copy of the slides, which meant you could follow along with the instructor on either the screen or your handout. Herein lies the dilemma: The school must teach certain basic information to the student and the presentation of the information must be consistent for each campus. Putting a block of text on a screen is one way to do it, but is it the only way? A challenge that a technical school faces is how to present complex material to students in a way that both teaches and engages the students. I am not sure that PowerPoint slides are particularly successful in this regard, and they may no longer be the best medium for presenting this material. Recognize that many UTI students are in their teens or early twenties. They are millennials, or even Gen Z, and they are very savvy regarding social media, video, and various interactive platforms for communicating with each other. At some point, UTI may want to consider expanding the media platforms it employs in order to teach the lecture material more effectively.

In 2010, UTI began offering a program called Automotive Technology II, or "Tech 2," as an alternative format to the class lecture and lab schedule that I took. Tech 2 is a blended learning format that combines daily instructor-led theory and lab training with web-based learning. Students watch lectures online, from their homes, and take their 10-point multiple-choice tests online. They then go to the campus for the lab portions of their courses, meaning they spend less time at school. Tech 2 is currently offered at most other UTI campuses, but not at the one I attended.

A few of our instructors mentioned the inclusion of Tech 2 at other campuses, and indicated that UTI was considering whether to extend Tech 2 to our campus. Some students were excited about the possibility of not having to come to school for six hours a day and instead view the online course lectures within the comfort of their own homes. I ran into one UTI student who was a transfer from the Orlando campus of UTI, which has Tech 2. He said he much preferred Tech 2 because he thought the online lectures were much better than the in-person lectures he received from his instructors at my campus. I personally prefer the current format over Tech 2 because I like having the ability to ask questions directly to the instructors as the material is presented and get an immediate response. I suspect I would not learn as much if I were not in a classroom environment for the lectures. But then I am part of a different generation from most UTI students. I am probably showing my age here.

One area of routine focus in every course is safety. I think UTI does a great job promoting safety for those working on cars and trucks in the workplace as well as in school. In every course the instructor stressed the safe way to perform repairs, use tools, handle toxic or caustic liquids, and avoid personal injuries or damage to vehicles. Some instructors had funny stories of techs who took shortcuts and injured themselves (never fatally!) or who ignored the safety protocols. Every instructor uses the SOPs as another opportunity to cover, exhaustively, the safety requirements to observe when at UTI. These include oil-resistant and slip-resistant work boots and shoes, safety glasses during lab, and uniforms tucked in so they don't get caught in moving machinery—to name a few. We are also taught how to identify and locate all fire extinguishers, eye wash stations, and first aid kits in each of the labs. We are taught how to exit the school in the event of a fire and the rally point where we are supposed to meet up in the parking lot. The instructors also covered related topics such as where to go in the event of a tornado and what to do in the event of an "active shooter" situation. I give the school a lot of credit for its repeated emphasis on workplace and school safety.

There is room for improvement in the safety training, however. One of the lab sheets we had to complete for each course was the Lab Safety Sheet. It asked questions about what safety apparel a tech should wear, what eye protection was recommended, what injuries could result from the improper use of hand tools, what injuries could result from the improper use of power tools, what federal and state rules applied to the safe handling, storage, and disposal of toxic chemicals and waste, and the location of the fire extinguishers in the lab. It also included miscellaneous "What other risks for potential injury could occur in the workplace?" types of questions. All of these questions are good ones, with the answers to each outlined in chapter three of our Course Book.

However, the Lab Safety Sheet in every course is the same sheet with the same questions. So the students are never challenged by new questions. Students merely have to repeat the same answers they put down in the previous course. Some students took a photo on their cellphones of their completed Lab Safety Sheet from a prior course and simply copied it for the next course. Completing the Lab Safety Sheet was considered to be just "busy work" to finish and submit by the end of the day. More "pencil whipping." I would have expected that the Lab Safety Sheet would be customized for each course. That is, the questions on each sheet would reflect the specific material that would be covered in each course. That way, the Lab Safety Sheet you fill out for Basic Engines, for example, where you are working only with hand tools on engines with no fluids, would be different from the one you would fill out for Climate Control, where you are handling R-134a refrigerant. Instead, I filled out the exact same Lab Safety Sheet for every single one of my seventeen courses.

Another component of the routine at UTI is the morning break (fifteen minutes) and the lunch break (thirty minutes). I am grateful that UTI incorporated these breaks into our schedule because they gave me an opportunity to stretch my legs, walk around a little bit, and get through what is otherwise a long sit for me (especially given my bad back). The food offerings at UTI were subpar and a few ambitious students would drive off campus to a fast-food restaurant to get something to eat during the lunch break. I say "ambitious" because the restaurants were not close to campus, leaving students with just a few minutes before lunch break was over to wolf down their food. When I first started at UTI, we had a little café called "The Pit Stop" that served breakfast and lunch. It was run by a local food services company that also served local schools and hospitals. Halfway through the school year, the food services company terminated the contract, claiming it was not making enough money—so the Pit Stop closed. As limited as the food choices were beforehand, they got demonstrably worse after that. Our choices were either vending machine food, or ... *wait for it ... wait for it ...* pizza—provided by a pizza truck that came to the school every day. I brought my own lunch with me every day. *I'm old school.*

UTI offered almost no organized activities during lunch. Occasionally the school has a Student Appreciation Day, which involves games and similar activities during an extended lunch period. This event would occur about once every three months. But other than that, lunch was always free time or "downtime" for the students and the instructors. While I understand that instructors and students appreciate free time, I wonder if students would be better served if they could elect to attend a supplemental learning presentation during the lunch break. Subjects could extend beyond what is taught in class. I am reminded of the "Lunch and Learn" programs we used to do at the law firm on changes in the law or marketing for lawyers or legal writing, etc. I imagine such extension programs would translate well to a technical school, where there are so many interesting topics to cover. For example, I often heard other students complain about how hard it was for them to remove a stuck engine bolt when they were at work. Years of rust and improper threading often were the culprits. These students were not sure how to remove the rusted bolt and often had to ask others in the shop for advice. Why couldn't the school put on a short presentation on how to remove rusted bolts, such as how to apply heat to a bolt with a torch to free it? Or as another topic, what are the shortcuts for testing for a misfiring spark plug (e.g., ever see a tech put a screwdriver into an ignition wire to see if it is working)? This variation on "Lunch and Learn" could consist of practical demonstrations where one of the instructors gives the students some insights and "how-to's" on a topic or shop-related situation that is common to all technicians. This practical know-how from the instructors could benefit every student. Or what if there was a presentation by a visiting service manager from a local car dealership demonstrating some new tool to make car repair easier? There are an almost unlimited number of topics that could be covered in a "Lunch and Learn" format to provide practical training that is not otherwise covered in any of the courses. UTI would not have to offer these programs frequently. Even providing it once a month or once every two months might make the lunch break a little more interesting and provide some valuable and practical supplemental knowledge.

Another thing that UTI does exceptionally well is helping students find employment. UTI tries very hard to place every student into a tech job, and the employment department is particularly proactive in this regard. UTI wants students to acquire a job while they are in school, and it helps students with the interview process for jobs after graduation. This emphasis on job procurement is understandable given that UTI is a technical school, but I think, more importantly, UTI wants students to know that they have support in their job search. Students are not left up to their own devices to muddle through finding work on their own. The employment team visits classes frequently and may interrupt instructors, mid-lecture, to talk about job opportunities and upcoming job fairs. They even provide school-wide programs where prospective employers and former students who were successfully placed in desirable jobs address the students, giving them encouragement and offering insight into what they should do to ensure their success in the job market. There is a special presentation on how to prepare a resumé and students are assisted one-on-one with the preparation of their own resumés. Towards the end of my program, we attended a presentation by the employment department featuring an HR director of a local trucking company. She gave us a "Do's and Don'ts" lecture with some helpful tips on how to go into an interview and come out with a job offer. *Do*: Ask questions about the job and the work you would do. *Don't*: Wear shorts and a T-shirt to the interview. *Do*: Research the company and make it clear you know about the company and what it does. *Don't*: Bring your family to the interview . . .

The school has numerous motivational posters mounted in the hallways to inspire students. One includes a photo of a V-8 engine with the caption *"The fire in its belly matches THE FIRE IN YOURS."* Another one features a mammoth semi tractor-trailer and states *"Let others climb the corporate ladder. You'll take the HYDRAULIC LIFT."* On each floor of the school, near the central staircase, a massive floor-length mirror showcases an overhead sign that reads *"Would you hire this person?"*

Interestingly enough, the major focus for prospective employers is not the students' grades, but their attendance. Employers give UTI a lot of credit for teaching the basics. They figure that graduates of UTI probably can be taught everything that a tech needs to know in order to be successful at the workplace. In other words, UTI graduation is a badge of *trainability*. However, employers don't want to deal with people who are no-shows. They don't want to hire someone who has a poor record of attendance at UTI, because that record suggests this individual may not show up to work every day. Attendance is so essential at UTI that it factors highly into whether you pass a course. You must have at least a seventy percent attendance record for the course to pass it. Notwithstanding, it does not look good on your school resumé if it reflects that you attended UTI courses only seventy percent of the time—even if you pass the course. So, the employment department consistently harps on the attendance metric for the students and exhorts everyone to achieve an excellent or perfect attendance record. That way, employers will consider them as viable job candidates. The importance of attendance is highlighted in lectures on a weekly—if not daily—basis at UTI. Seventy percent attendance translates into a student missing up to twelve hours of class time and lab time without failing the course. This twelve-hour cutoff is firm. If a student misses more than twelve hours of class time and lab time, he or she will fail the course. Twelve hours of time adds up to roughly two days of classes. A student who misses more than twelve hours of class and thus fails the course is said to have "houred out." It happened in almost every one of my courses.

During my year at UTI, the school hosted a number of job fairs for students. Some focused exclusively on auto-related jobs and some were limited to diesel-related jobs (e.g., trucks, busses, train engines, industrial). Not surprisingly, given the current demand, there were far more diesel employers than auto employers attending the campus job fairs, hoping to attract students to work for them. I was surprised that no information about the job fairs was provided to students in advance, other than variations of "We are going to have a job fair next Tuesday." I would have expected the employment department to distribute a list of employers expected to attend so students could see in advance who was going to be there and identify which companies might interest them. Advance information could also include whether the companies have previously hired UTI students or whether they are participating for the first time. Without this information, students were often left to wander the auditorium, walking by each table, in order to discover which companies had representatives in attendance. I am sure that many students, given their age, have no idea who many of these companies are and cannot determine from a name alone whether a company might be of interest to them. Some advance information on each of the companies would have been helpful. Job fairs take place during class time, so it is a waste of precious class time to send the students into the auditorium without any preparation or advance knowledge of which companies will be participating.

Given the focus on courses, training, and employment, there is no extracurricular activity at UTI. A UTI student council meets once every few weeks for lunch between the morning and afternoon sessions. The student council is run by current students who volunteer to serve on it. They don't have any real power. They can make suggestions, however. For example, at their suggestion, the school installed wall clocks in each of the classrooms. Students are encouraged to attend the meetings with the offer of a free lunch, consisting of—*of course*—pizza. Rogers (who showed up for the free pizza so often, they invited him to join as a member) shared with me that the student council did nothing more than listen to students' gripes about the school and certain instructors.

UTI also offers peer-to-peer tutoring after school for those students who want additional help. A few of the smarter students were designated as tutors and provided one-on-one tutoring in classrooms reserved for this purpose. Given the difficulty a number of students had in the electronics courses, a special tutor assigned to each of those courses would show up before and after class to answer any questions.

Other than these specific additions to the base education, there are no car clubs, special interest groups, or any attempt by the school to create a sense of camaraderie among the students through affinity groups. In this way, technical school is very different from a four-year college. There was one notable exception: one classroom was set aside to serve as a lounge for veterans, so I expect that a number of veterans met there from time to time, and thus, were able to forge some new friendships. I suspect most students simply do not have time for any extracurricular clubs or other group activities. Given their financial needs, they often have to go directly to work once class is dismissed and cannot afford to spend any additional time on campus.

Despite the busy schedule of a technical school, at times as a student I found myself sitting in class with nothing to do. I was surprised by this lull in activity when it first occurred, and I never really got used to it. There were times of the day, such as when we returned to the classroom from lab (either before lunch or at the end of the day), when the instructor had no planned activity other than waiting for the bell. Because I was so gung-ho about school and learning, I did not fully appreciate that some occasional "free" time might be in order for both students and instructors alike. In addition, on the final Friday of each course, there is often some "downtime" while you are waiting to take the 20-point final test before being dismissed for the day. In many courses, unless the instructor offered a special course review in preparation for the 20-point final test, we would just sit and chat until it was time to take the test. In some cases, we sat for almost two hours. Sometimes the instructor stipulated that the final Friday would be spent "cleaning up the lab," but that rarely occurred, or only took fifteen minutes to complete. A few courses featured an actual lecture on the final Friday, but that was rare. In almost all the courses, we were required to finish all our labs by the final Thursday, the day of our lab final, so we did not have any lab work to complete on that Friday. Accordingly, final Fridays were a long sit. One instructor used this free time as an opportunity to show a lengthy video featuring a motivational speaker giving a convention audience tips on how to succeed in business. Another instructor shared with the class his personal photos on his computer of his various cars. Others replayed an episode from an old car show on TV. Yeah, it was that kind of day on the final Friday. A lot of us became easily bored, waiting to take the final test.

The final Friday also featured something that completely astonished me. It is called the "one-test retake." At this particular campus, UTI students can elect to retake any one test they took previously during the course—other than the 20-point final test—in order to attempt to improve their class points score and perhaps also their grade. As I described previously, the instructor reviews every 10-point test immediately after collecting the answer sheets and provides the correct answers. Accordingly, if you pay attention during the test review, you will be able to memorize the correct answers. The purpose of the one-test retake is to help those students who are really struggling or those who for some reason just blew a particular test (perhaps because they missed a day of class). Almost all of my friends elected to take the one-test retake in one of their courses, and some of them did it in every course. In this way, they could put some additional points back up on the board. The one-test retake occurs once the 20-point final is completed and collected in class. Those students who wish to do a one-test retake hang out in the hallway until the instructor returns with the retakes. Accordingly, on the final Friday of every course, as I headed out to the parking lot to drive home, it was common to see students congregating outside of every classroom, waiting to do the one-test retake.

I was astonished by this practice because I have never encountered it before. I have never known a school to offer a student a "do-over" on a test, the academic equivalent of a mulligan[23] in golf. I can only speculate on the reasoning for this practice. I suppose for some students the classroom portion of technical school is a difficult experience. They may not be well suited to classroom learning and thus they may struggle, not just in one class, but through the entire program. Or, for some, it could be that English may not be their first language, making it exceptionally difficult for them to navigate the written tests. I also wonder if the one-test retake is an admission that technical school is in fact difficult for many students and some form of "assistance" is necessary to ensure some students pass courses, graduate, and get a job. In any case, the one-test retake can be a lifeline. It gives these students a second chance.

The friends I knew who did one-test retakes did not seem to struggle in school, with maybe one or two exceptions. In almost all the cases of which I was aware, they elected a one-test retake on a test where they had gotten a very low score and wanted a 10 to pull up their GPA. One of my friends disclosed that he raised his grade for one class from a B to an A as a result of the one-test retake. Neither Rogers nor I ever did a one-test retake. The rule is that if you do a one-test retake, you automatically become ineligible for SOC. Our motivation for avoiding the one-test retake was not because of that disqualification, however. It was because we almost always did pretty well on the 10-point tests. Retaking one test to gain an extra point or two was not going to make any difference in our grades. And in my case, well, I just did not think it was right to retake a test. I just could not get used to the idea. It was to me a mild form of cheating. And, frankly, I could live with my test result, whatever it was.

There was an interesting one-test retake incident involving my friend, Gordon, the aspiring tech I previously mentioned who had

---

23   A mulligan is a second chance to perform an action, usually after the first chance went wrong through bad luck or a blunder. (*Wikipedia*, n.d.).

easily defeated the tracking device his parents put on his car in high school. Gordon and I sat next to each other in one particular course, and we were in the same lab group. Gordon was doing pretty well in the course, but he did poorly on one or two of the 10-point tests. The instructor was not particularly punctual in returning our lab scores to us during the course and, on our final Friday, we had no inkling of what our lab final grades were—or even our overall lab grades. So, we take the 20-point final test on the final Friday. I head home immediately after the test, as always. Gordon remains behind. He had received a 7 out of 10 on a previous test and wanted to do a one-test retake to try to raise his score. After the 20-point final test, he took the one-test retake and then he returned home, but he was still in the dark as to his score on his lab final and his overall score in lab. The instructor had still not completed all of the grading at the time Gordon took his retest. Gordon returned to school the following week, where he is elated to learn that he earned SOC for the course. But then he realizes, *Wait a minute, I took a one-test retake. How the hell did that happen? Everyone knows that if you do a one-test retake you cannot earn SOC.* It is something the instructors cover during the SOPs in every course. Gordon wisely did not attempt to clarify this apparent discrepancy with the instructor, not wanting to "look a gift horse in the mouth." He just basked in the glory of his SOC status and we celebrated with him.

Later that week, we figured out what must have occurred. From his progress report he eventually received, Gordon learned he earned a perfect score in lab for the entire course. That feat put him in the running for SOC, but he was completely unaware of his lab score on the final Friday because the instructor had not yet published it. So even though the one-test retake should have disqualified Gordon, we theorize that the instructor realized that Gordon had no way of knowing that he was in the running for SOC at the time because of the instructor's delay in grading labs. In other words, the instructor realized the mistake was his own "My Bad" (*Sorry, Mr. M*), and thus gave SOC to Gordon because Gordon had done nothing wrong. That's the best way we can explain it. *Truth is stranger than fiction*. But I am happy that Gordon got SOC. He deserved it.

CHAPTER 5

WHO ARE THOSE GUYS?

Before I decided to enroll in UTI, I attended an open house held on a Saturday. The open house was attended by prospective students and their parents, and the auditorium must have been filled with at least two hundred people. The presentation to the group in the auditorium was mercifully brief, with one or two slick videos. The presenter had a senior position in admissions and outlined the requirements for admission, some basic information on the program, and data on job placement after graduation. We were then divided into small groups so we could tour the campus and observe classrooms firsthand. The admissions guy divided us into tour groups according to age. He said, "Okay, the first group will meet by the door and will be taken around by Mr. J." We all turned to see Mr. J wave his hand. The admissions guy continued. "For this first group, let's have everyone who is over the age of . . . *twenty*." If it wasn't obvious before, it was crystal clear at that moment that UTI's entering class was *a lot* younger than me. The 20+ age group consisted of me and four or five other prospective students and their parents. The entire room looked at me as I stood up and joined the first tour group. They must have assumed I was someone's father. I really did not care. But *twenty? Really?*

The first UTI instructor I met on the tour was Mr. T, who gave us a presentation in the lab for Power & Performance (a course where students are taught that the power and performance of a car can be improved without affecting its tailpipe emissions). The lab was a large space that included a number of cars, lifts, and toolboxes, and several rooms with dynamometers.[24] The cars included a newer Camaro and an older Mustang. Mr. T gave us an overview of the course. We would remove certain car parts, like the air intake system or exhaust system, bolt on certain aftermarket performance-improvement parts, and then put the modified car on a dyno to determine how much additional horsepower and torque the engine would now make. *Whoa! Who could resist that?* I was hooked, and from that moment I knew I wanted to attend UTI. Mr. T was full of energy. You could tell he was passionate about the subject matter because he smiled as he talked. For me, that is always a "tell."

Later, when Mr. T was my instructor for the Power & Performance course, I learned of his special interest in modifying cars for drag racing. He loved driving fast, just like many UTI students—even on the street. Mr. T would often say that he drove faster than any UTI student. I don't recall anyone in class challenging him to prove that bold statement. However, his stories in class about the modifications he made to his drag racing car (an older Dodge SRT[25]) were really interesting to me. He was once stopped by the local police for driving his SRT on the street because the car was too loud. It had a muffler, but it was a performance muffler so the engine roared at a high decibel level. At traffic court, Mr. T was able to beat the ticket because he could demonstrate that when he bought the car from the

24 Also referred to as a "dyno," it is a machine that consists of a huge roller built into the floor, often in a separate room. The car is strapped down to the floor with the drive wheels of the car (front or rear) resting on the roller. As the car accelerates, the amount of force needed to turn the roller is determined and a computer translates the information into horsepower and torque.

25 "SRT" stands for "Street & Racing Technology," and is the high performance line of cars built by Dodge (now part of Fiat Chrysler Automobiles).

dealer, it came from the manufacturer with no muffler on it at all. That was the way they were made by Dodge. Mr. T had the documentation to prove it and showed it to the judge. He also showed the judge that he himself had installed an aftermarket muffler on the car in order to reduce the noise. Accordingly, the judge dismissed the case. *Kind of arbitrary, right?*

The second instructor I met on the tour was Mr. O, who was stationed in the Toyota Lab. UTI offers manufacturer-specific training as an add-on to the basic curriculum. The Toyota-specific training qualifies the student to work in either a Toyota or Lexus dealership. It is fairly popular with UTI students, given that there are so many Toyota and Lexus cars currently on the roads. A number of my friends, including Valdez and Temple, opted for this extra education. Mr. O was the *LOUDEST* instructor I had at UTI. When we were on the open house tour, I simply assumed that he was shouting so his voice could reach everyone on the tour. When I had him as an instructor, I surmised that he was loud on purpose to keep people from falling asleep in class. He had a great sense of humor and told a lot of jokes about working in the shop and his own personal journey from technician to Master Certified Technician[26] to UTI instructor. Mr. O is a very smart technician. I learned that he passed all eight of his ASE[27] certification tests on the same day and on his first try. That has to be a record of sorts.

Mr. O was my instructor for a course entitled Drivability and Emissions. It is a fascinating course, brimming with technical

---

26   An ASE Certified Technician becomes a Master Certified Technician after earning all eight of the specific testing certification areas.

27   The National Institute for Automotive Service Excellence (ASE) is a professional certification group that certifies professionals and shops in the automotive repair and service industry. Techs are certified if they pass a test in an area of specialization, including Engine Repair, Automatic Transmissions, Suspension & Steering, and Brakes, to name a few.

information regarding the components of the car's emissions system and how they work. Mr. O is a gifted artist as well as technician. He can freehand any component in a car in three dimensions, in different colors, and with labels and arrows showing movement or direction. What's more, he can do this while describing the component and its operation and interspersing the lecture with comments about what his girlfriend is going to make for dinner that night. *This is not an exaggeration.* He is the consummate multitasker. All the other instructors know of his artistic abilities. A number of them attempted to draw pictures on the board (some were better than others) and apologetically prefaced their attempts with a disclaimer: "Well, I am not Mr. O, but here's a drawing of how this component works . . ." One of my friends referred to him as "Picasso," but it was not until I had Mr. O as an instructor that I fully appreciated his skillset as an instructor and an artist. He would occasionally take up to twenty minutes of class time drawing an entire system on the board. I would often try to duplicate his drawing in my notes to get the full value of it. My weak attempts, however—even with his drawing as a reference—could never compare to his high-quality renderings.

During my yearlong program at UTI, I was taught by fifteen different instructors. I took seventeen courses, but two of the instructors taught me in more than one course. There are several more instructors I befriended in passing because they substituted in my class for a few days or were kind enough to say "hello" to me in the hallway. The instructors are extremely knowledgeable and experienced in the automotive industry. They possess a wide variety of experiences working for dealerships and independent shops as technicians, service advisors, service managers, and ultimately as UTI instructors. Their understanding of how cars work covers Ford, Toyota, Nissan, Audi, GM, Dodge, Chrysler, and Volvo, to name but a few of the manufacturers. Almost all of them have fifteen years or more of experience working in the field (with a number amassing twenty-plus years) and most of them have been teaching at UTI for an extended period (over ten years). A couple of them are UTI graduates themselves. One, Mr. G, admitted that while he was attending UTI, he'd had another of my instructors, Mr. N, for an instructor *back in the day.*

I joked with my lawyer friends before retirement that I assumed I would share more in common with the instructors at UTI than with the students, again taking into account the age difference between me and the other UTI students. It is certainly true that I am closer in age to the instructors than to the students. Sometimes, an instructor would make references to older cars, older technology, or older television shows during a lecture and then look at me or say, "Mr. Ellis, you remember that. Don't you?" Occasional references to "Y2K" would be combined with an instructor's inevitable glance in my direction, since most of the students were born in 2000 or perhaps one or two years prior and thus had no idea what "Y2K" meant.

However, other than being somewhat close in age, I really shared nothing else in common with the instructors. I did not have the same credentials they had. I did not possess the experience they did. I knew nothing about the subject matter; they knew so much. I was not in any way, shape, or form their peer. They were the instructors. I was only a student, trying to learn.

Another marked difference is that many of the instructors entered the automotive industry at a young age, like most of my fellow UTI students, and worked their way up over years of hard work and experience. In that way, the instructors had more in common with the other UTI students than with me. Their stories of how they worked the less-desirable entry-level jobs in the shop before advancing to the more-desirable jobs must have resonated with the other UTI students who desired a similar career path. Most of the UTI instructors had attended a technical school or a community college to gain some training before entering the workforce. Many have fathers, uncles, brothers or other relatives in the automotive repair business who mentored them and gave them advice. They share this legacy with many of the students at UTI.

In general, the instructors shared with the students a lot of information, not only about the automotive world, but about themselves personally. They were very open with students when it came to their own career paths, their personal challenges, their illnesses, their marriages or family difficulties, or whatever was on their minds. I am not by nature a "sharing person" when it comes to personal information, so I was not entirely comfortable with the degree to which instructors shared personal details with the class. For instance, as a student, I heard about *every* instructor's divorce. *I mean every one.* It was invariably described as a "bitter divorce." This information usually came out during the SOPs, when the instructor shared a few details about himself as an introduction to the class. One instructor referred to his ex as his "starter wife." To be honest, I was not prepared for the frequent references to divorce. At one point, I'd heard about so many instructor divorces I just assumed that divorce was a necessary casualty of working in the industry. However, to be fair, I am not sure about the statistics. As over 50% of married couples divorce these days, it very well could be that the instructor population is no different from any other demographic group in American society.

As a further example of this "personal sharing" by instructors, one instructor informed the class that his daughter had been sexually assaulted by a boy at high school and that the school did nothing to punish the boy. Instead, the school punished his daughter. The incident was clearly very painful to the instructor and he was understandably traumatized by it. However, the instructor spared us no detail about it, from the incident itself to its aftermath, the confrontation between his daughter and the boy's girlfriend (in which the girlfriend accused his daughter of lying), the countless meetings at school with the principal, and how his daughter was trying to cope with it. As a father I was extremely moved and upset about this matter, but I could not tell if the instructor was sharing it with us to garner sympathy or whether he simply wanted to vent his frustrations. I could not tell if the other students shared my reaction of sympathy and concern. No one around me seemed to be rattled by his recounting. No one mentioned it further or proclaimed, "Oh my God! That's terrible."

I was so moved that I wanted to approach the instructor after class and offer to find him a lawyer to help his daughter with her situation. But this instructor (like a number of UTI instructors) held a fairly negative view of lawyers, so I held back. I heard disparaging comments about lawyers from a number of UTI instructors during their lectures, even in instances when I suspected the instructor was aware that I was a lawyer. I did not take it personally. I knew they were just telling a joke (e.g., "car salesmen are the most distrusted group of people—next to lawyers") or simply venting. In most cases, the negativity stemmed from a "bitter divorce." One instructor complained about the $17,000 in legal fees he had to pay in connection with his divorce. He was apoplectic that his divorce cost him that amount of money in legal fees. He found the figure excessive and was no fan of lawyers because of it.

Several of my instructors are diabetics who ate constantly during class in order to maintain their blood sugar levels. One instructor kept a blood sugar monitor on him at all times. Whenever the monitor went off, he would leave the classroom to scour the vending machines for a snack. This meant he was gone from class for up to five or ten minutes, several times a week. Another instructor had an autoimmune disease, which may have caused him to stop working in the field. He was fairly young and had amassed roughly ten years of experience in the field before he began teaching at UTI. He often shared the challenges he faced getting his medications right.

One instructor was very hygiene-conscious and made no secret about it to us. We often devoted the end of his class to thoroughly spraying and wiping down the tables, which I actually appreciated. However, he also seemed obsessed with talking about shit. *Feces.* During SOPs he remarked that when people fart, they are actually spreading small fecal particles into the air (" . . . *so if you have to pass gas, please do so outside of the classroom"*). He shared a cautionary tale about a student several years earlier who tried pretending he was farting in class, but instead had actually shit his pants, leaving a small pile of brown matter on his chair. They evidently had to clear the classroom and call in a hazmat team to clean it up. *Seriously: This is what he told us during SOPs.* I had actually seen this same feces-obsessed instructor in the men's room several months prior to taking his course. At the time, I did not even know his name. But I do recall that while standing at the urinal he announced to every-one, "Ah yes, the sweet smell of UTI students on the throne during break." I am sure he thought he was simply being humorous. I just found it odd for an instructor to talk that way in the men's room. Perhaps he was just trying to joke around with the students and be "one of the guys." A number of instructors did try very hard to chat with and relate to students in a friendly, casual way. Those who were successful in this regard were popular with the students. I was lucky to have some of them as instructors. At the end of class they were often surrounded by students, answering questions about their cars or just shooting the breeze.

As students, we quickly became aware of each instructor's favor-ite car, what cars he owned, what cars he sold, and whether he was currently working on a project car. One instructor collected pinball machines. One instructor had several Harley Davidson motorcycles. One instructor mentioned his side business as a mechanic, stressing that he was looking for more customers and suggesting we dissem-inate his phone number to our friends and families. In fact, in that particular course, he focused so much of the discussion on his side business, there were days when I wondered whether we would ever cover any of the lecture material. One instructor was a long-distance runner and used to share with us how many miles he had run over the prior weekend. Another instructor built high-performance engines on the side and showed us photos of an engine he built for a car auctioned off for charity.

In addition, some of the instructors used the classroom as an opportunity to discuss their personal brand of politics, complain about "do-gooders" and "tree huggers," question aloud whether climate change was really a thing, or complain about local politicians or the government. I did not share all of their opinions, but I did not really mind that they shared them with the class. Everyone is entitled to their own views, especially when it comes to politics.

The students, on the other hand, rarely—if at all—brought up politics or expressed any political views. Midterm elections were held in 2018, but for these students, the elections may as well not have existed. Elections had no perceptible bearing on their lives and most students had no idea who was running for office, nor did they care. Similarly, there was no commentary at all on news or world events among UTI students. Students exclusively discussed cars, their jobs, finances, sex, money (or lack thereof), and the weather. The weather was perhaps the biggest topic of all, especially during the winter when there was a chance that school might be cancelled. I can recall only once when a major news event was brought up in class by a student. It was after the Tree of Life synagogue shooting in Pittsburgh where eleven people were killed and seven were injured by a gunman. It was a horrific antisemitic event that made front-page headlines for days. I overheard one student in my Automatic Transmission course, Anders, bring it up to one of his friends, Stein, during a break.

Anders asked, "Stein, what about Pittsburgh?"

Stein paused for a while, then replied, "What do you mean?"

Anders shook his head. "Bro, they were your peeps."

Stein paused for a little while more, then finally said, "That's fucked up." And that was the end of the discussion.

A couple of instructors crossed the line a number of times with inappropriate comments, particularly when it came to the subject of women. One instructor advised us not to date UTI girls. He never explained why. He just said not to date them. Since women were not present in the vast majority of my classes, there was the occasional sexual reference to the shapes or parts of women's bodies. I could understand juvenile comments coming from the students, but in this case they were coming from some of the instructors. One instructor made a common "jerking-off" gesture when describing what someone did at home instead of studying. I suspect much of this behavior would not occur if there were women in the classroom, but I cannot be certain. A female student was actually in the classroom when the one instructor referred to his ex-wife as his "starter wife." *What was she supposed to think when he said that?* That instructor's statement really bothered me. I considered finding a moment when I could ask the female student, privately in the hallway, her thoughts about that comment. But then again, I did not want to put her on the spot and confront her with what she might perceive as my *expecting* her to react to what must be very common in technical school—sexism. I did not want to make her feel uncomfortable, so I never did ask her about it. Another instructor, who was contemplating retirement in a few years, often made off-color and inappropriate comments. He then immediately followed each such comment with, "Yes, I know I am politically incorrect. But what are they going to do? *Fire me?*"

I suspect that the way instructors talk in class is similar to the way technicians talk at work. In other words, they talk the same way they would talk if they were working with other techs in the service department of a dealer or on the shop floor. Their choice of language and the stories they shared in some way gave me a glimpse into "life as a tech." I will be the first to admit that perhaps I am overly sensitive about language because I was not exposed to such discourse in my previous career as a lawyer. Our use of language in my law firm office and with clients was much different. The offensive language used by the some of the instructors would doubtlessly be deemed inappropriate for my former workplace, but I also think this language is inappropriate for any workplace. I have to admit there were times I wanted to shout out, "Inappropriate!" when I heard these types of comments from the instructors. Instead, I simply muttered under my breath. I did not feel like taking them on in front of the other students.

I also did not want to be singled out or attract unwanted attention. As the instructors are given complete control and autonomy over the classroom, like most teachers, their word becomes the rule of law and students are very aware of it. However, I would prefer each of them to act more like role models for the students who (due to their young age) may not know what is appropriate to say and what is not. Of course, not every instructor made inappropriate comments. A number of my instructors were perfect examples of how to teach and never crossed the line, or even approached it. They were able to effectively build rapport with students without making any off-color remarks, so I know it can be done. And though UTI is a technical school and not a four-year college, I would like to think the instructors are well aware of the tremendous impact they have on eighteen- and nineteen-year-olds who are still easily influenced by what they see and hear.

I give the instructors a lot of credit for embracing the challenges of teaching at a technical school for young men and women who are learning a complicated field like automotive technology while struggling to make ends meet. Every single one of my instructors was outgoing and friendly to students; talked with them about cars, jobs, school, and the automotive industry; and showed a passion for the subject matter. It was clear the instructors loved working on cars and were proud of the experience they had accumulated while working in the field. And yet, passion and experience alone are not enough to manage a classroom of eighteen- and nineteen-year-olds. Each instructor has to acquire a new set of skills for teaching at UTI. For the most part, I think the instructors I had successfully learned these new skills. For example, I witnessed only two instances when students were sent home for sleeping in class—despite the SOPs hammering into us the prohibition against doing it. I thought the instructors did a great job of balancing the goal of getting the class through the instructional material and the need for cautioning students to stay awake or not be disruptive in class. Over a few months of teaching, I am sure any new UTI instructor is exposed to an array of behaviors and develops a strategy for what is important to call out and what can slide. One of the goals of UTI is not only to teach a heavy technical curriculum to the students, but also to give students an opportunity to graduate and become successful technicians. While there are plenty of rules at UTI, if every single infraction was called out, many students would fail courses and not complete the program. I suspect the instructors know the risk associated with being overly strict disciplinarians. It would make it much more difficult for students to progress through the program if every "foot fault" were called out by the instructor. Accordingly, each instructor devises his or her own system for enforcing the rules in class, including when to bring down the hammer on a student and when to let an infraction slide. Every instructor's value system is different. Some are pretty tough, some are not. I found that I could easily figure out during the SOPs on the first day of a course how tolerant an instructor was going to be during the course.

One of my instructors, a disciplinarian, would immediately start with attendance the moment the bell sounded at the beginning of class. Students who were running late, but whose last names began with letters at the end of the alphabet, could sometimes manage arriving a minute or two late to class and be safely in their seats before their names were called. Students whose last names began with A or B were not so fortunate. Other instructors would simply circulate the sign-in sheet when the bell rang. As long as you were in your seat before the sign-in sheet completed its course around the room and was returned to the instructor, you were safe. Some instructors were constantly reminding certain students to tuck in their shirts, wear their ID badges on the outside of their clothes, or take off their non-UTI jackets or other apparel. Other instructors never said a word about uniforms. One instructor who was always very entertaining and made a lot of jokes in class when delivering his lectures, gave the false impression he would not be a rules enforcer. However, it turned out he really was a stickler for attendance and uniform violations even though he rarely called someone out in class. One of my friends noticed several of these infractions on his progress report and asked this particular instructor about them. I overheard the instructor explain, "Yeah, you know you were late two days last week. I did not say anything to you, but I made a note of it on my records." I guess the instructor did not like public confrontations.

On the opposite extreme, I also had a few instructors who were exceptionally loose and lax in their enforcement of the rules. In one course, the instructor did not monitor the room during test taking. This instructor was in stark contrast to most other instructors who watched the class like hawks, walking up and down the aisles to ensure no one was talking, skimming a neighbor's score sheet, or searching online for answers on a cell phone. Instead, this instructor remained glued to his computer screen at his desk for the duration of every test, never looking up. During one of the 10-point tests, I finished and turned in mine, then glanced around the room to see who was still working on theirs. As sometimes occurred, I finished before many of the other students and simply wanted to gauge how long I would have to wait until everyone else turned in their tests. In this particular instance, I noticed one student at the very back of the room, head down on his arm on the table, scanning the cell phone he held under the table as he worked on his test. *Really, Bro?* The instructor, eyes affixed to his computer screen, never even noticed.

This same instructor also had the "generous" habit of providing the class with the answer to one of the ten questions on the test the day before administering the 10-point test. The question was usually the "self-study" question, taken directly from the Course Book chapter that accompanied almost every lecture. Sometimes he would simply identify the question, and sometimes he would even go a step further and give us the answer. *Yes, this really happened.*

Another instructor had absolutely no control over behavior in the classroom. In this course, the nature of the lab assignment often required the instructor to be physically present at one clip car[28] at a time so he could ensure the students correctly performed the steps to measure the performance of a component. Thus, the instructor's attention was solely focused on the activity at one clip car at a time. He could not monitor students in the other lab groups who were still awaiting their turns for him to come over. As a result, a few students used this waiting time to play around with the clip cars, honk the horns, rev the engines, goof off, and generally joke around. I am ashamed to admit that my lab group in this course was one that liked to play around when the instructor was not watching. I often found

---

28   A "clip car" is the front half of a car, modified so it can be used in the lab as a teaching tool. UTI gets its clip cars from a company that produces them. These cars start out as actual cars, but they are damaged by hurricanes or other natural disasters and thus are junked by insurance companies. The clip car is suspended above the ground on a frame and has a working engine, front wheels, a dashboard, two front seats, a steering wheel, pedals, a modified gas tank, and an exhaust. There usually are no doors on the car and no windows, windshield, or roof. The engine works, the wheels turn (most are front-wheel-drive cars), the headlights and turn signals work, the air-conditioning works, and—in some cases—the radio, too.

myself maneuvering away from them towards the opposite side of the lab in order to disassociate myself from their antics. If the instructor did take notice, I did not want to be there to catch the heat. Luckily, the instructor never did call them out. They were never sanctioned for their juvenile behavior.

This type of behavior spilled over to the classroom as well. Whenever the instructor left the room following a lecture, for example to go into the lab to prepare it for our next lab assignment, the classroom often exploded with horseplay. Again, it was the other guys in my lab group who were the offenders. They took advantage of the instructor's absence to take components off of the instructor's desk and hide them in students' backpacks, clip pens and other items to the collars of students who were sleeping in class, and rearrange chairs. Again, I just walked away. Often, I moved to the back of the classroom when they started up. I did not want to be a part of these activities. Whenever the instructor re-entered the classroom, he seemed to ignore many of the pranks that had been pulled, and he never really did anything to stem the classroom misbehavior. This particular instructor is very bright and has taught for a number of years, so he was probably very aware of the class's hijinks. I figured he simply chose to ignore them because he must have felt it was pointless to try to corral these behaviors. *Boys will be boys.* Although he sometimes reprimanded some of the students for uniform violations, I don't think he ever actually wrote up anyone for an infraction.

Interestingly enough, it was in this same course that several students were expelled as a result of random drug testing. Drug testing is routine in the auto industry. If you are involved in an accident or injured while working in the shop, you are subsequently drug tested to determine if you were high or were on any illegal substances that may have contributed to the accident. The school does not pull someone out of class for drug testing unless the student shows suspicious behavior, another student or instructor notifies the

administration about a concern about a particular student, or something else indicates that the student is taking illegal drugs. Although
I don't know for certain, the rumor was that these particular students
were tested because someone had told on them—perhaps having
observed them getting high while on break. In any event, the penalty
is severe for any student who tests positive for illegal drugs. That
student flunks the course, is suspended from the program, and after
a certain amount of time must reapply and subsequently pass a drug
test in order to re-enroll. The students who were expelled were not in
my lab group, and I don't know if they ever returned to school. The
instructor never mentioned their absence from the course. I learned
everything through one of my friends who knew them.

The instructors prefer not to fail students, in part because they
are genuinely interested in their students' success. Instructors are also
acutely aware of their own track record for failing students. More
than one instructor mentioned to the class their failure rates for a
particular course, a statistic that seemed to carry a certain amount
of weight among the instructors.[29] While no one outright confirmed
it at the time, I suspected the instructors' own performance reviews
included this data point. Instructors monitored test scores and lab
scores closely and usually informed the class after every test whether
most people did well or poorly on that test. One time, the instructor
told us that not one person in the class scored a 10 on a particular
test—an extremely rare event—and that the class average on that
test was only 77%. Since 70% is the minimum passing grade for a
course, we knew the class as a whole had not done very well on that
one test. I suspect that at least some students in that course opted for
a one-test retake as a result.

29   In a subsequent conversation I had with senior leadership at UTI, I did
confirm that an instructor's failure rate for a particular course is in fact part
of his or her own performance review. Failing too many students would likely
impact an instructor in a negative way.

My instructor for my Automatic Transmissions course started the first day of class with a warning, "Well, this course has the reputation of being a GPA-buster, so you will need to study extra hard." I was initially worried, but this same instructor also handed out review sheets to study before the test. As it turns out, if you paid attention to the answers on the review sheets, you would be able to answer 70–80% of the questions on the upcoming test. I suspect the review sheets were created by that instructor in order to help the students pass the course. He must have anticipated that without them, a lot of students were likely to struggle. The review sheets were a valuable tool for me, personally. I ended up doing very well in that course. Not every course included review sheets. Why some instructors passed out review sheets and others did not was a mystery to me. In my Climate Control course, where we studied air-conditioning systems in cars, I don't think I could have passed the course without the review sheets. Similarly, in all of my electronics courses, the review sheets were an invaluable resource and study guide for the 10-point tests.

Some instructors adopted the role of benevolent dictators in the classroom. The instructors could be hard asses if they wanted to be, but for the most part they were not. Instead, the instructors exhibited a high degree of professionalism (other than the random inappropriate comments) and, without exception, all of them possessed a great sense of humor. In a school setting, a sense of humor is priceless. In general, the instructors were interested in the students' success. However, given the sheer numbers of students passing through their courses in a year, instructors could not afford to follow the progress of each and every student. They wanted the students to learn, to get good grades, to get good jobs, and have successful careers. They often asked students about their part-time work, their side projects, or the modifications they were doing to their personal cars. I cannot remember a single time when an instructor declined to answer a student's question, even one that pertained to a student's own personal car or one in their family. Mr. V, my instructor in Manual Trans, is also a Ford instructor (for the Ford advanced training program). When I had a misfire in my 2000 Mustang, he suggested to me ways to test, remove, and replace various components that could be causing the misfire. In this way, the instructors were unfailingly generous with their time and selfless. They were *that committed* to the vocation of teaching.

I also witnessed instructors' great efforts at self-restraint in situations in which I was certain a student would be thrown out of class. In my Brakes course, for example, we had one student who was exceptionally loud and boisterous. He seemed nice enough on the first day of the course when he introduced himself to me. He informed me that he was a veteran with PTSD. That was the first time anyone had introduced himself to me that way. To emphasize his point, he jabbed his finger into my chest as he spoke. This same student once became upset in class as the instructor, Mr. L, reviewed the most recent test and shared the correct answers with the class. This particular student was convinced a different answer was the correct one based upon what he thought he had read in the Course Book. He immediately started to loudly rant, shouting about how "fucked up" the test was, how everyone cheated on tests, and how the school itself was "fucked up." The other students simply rolled their eyes at his behavior. A second student, exasperated with this outburst, told him to shut up.

"I'm not talking to you!" snapped the first student, mid-rant.

"Everyone in the class can't help but listen to you, Bro, when you are yelling like that," quipped the second student.

Mr. L remained very calm throughout this outburst. He allowed the first student to vent and say his piece. Mr. L. kept assuring this student, "It's okay . . . It's okay . . ." I know other instructors who would not have hesitated to throw this student out of class for ranting and raving. But not Mr. L. He was very cool. He suggested to the student that he meet with him at the end of class to go over the question together so Mr. L could provide him a longer, more detailed explanation of why the correct answer was the correct answer.

This same student later became very frustrated and began shouting during the Brakes lab final. He had made a mistake using the brake lathe, a machine that grinds smooth the inside of a brake drum. This student bellowed about how "fucked up" the lab, the course, and the school were—to the point where everyone took notice, wondering when he would be ejected from class. And since the Brakes lab was in a huge room that was shared with three other courses, lots of other students also took notice upon hearing this student's loud outburst. Even one of the Educational Managers (EM) showed up to investigate the ruckus. When an EM shows up, look out! They have the supreme authority to kick a student out of a class. Mr. L, however, was again very calm with the disruptive student, and again allowed him to vent. He engaged him very quietly, using a soft voice so no one else in class could hear what he was saying. Eventually, the student calmed down and the drama was over. Despite being loud and easily excitable, this particular student was nevertheless bright. He successfully completed the course. I saw him in the hallway during the next course cycle, and he shared that he had scored an "A" for the Brakes course. *Good for him*, I thought. But I give "props" to Mr. L and his ability to prevent an angry scenario from turning into something much worse, which could have negatively affected this student's ability to graduate.

As I previously mentioned, I was not very confident during lab finals. The pressure of completing a task before time expired proved too much for me to handle in a number of courses. I have always thought of myself as someone who is good under pressure, and that is what I always believed as a lawyer. But when it comes to working with my hands, my ability to beat the clock is not something I would bet on. And yet, I did pretty well overall at UTI. My lab grades were excellent, considering how stressful I found the lab finals. While I can pat myself on the back somewhat for "muscling through" these lab finals, I also credit several UTI instructors—perhaps sensing my frustration or fear or panic—who gave me a break when it came to lab finals.

In one instance, Mr. S, our Basic Electronics instructor, must have sensed my increasing stress level as he approached me to let me know I was at the halfway point of the lab final. We had to switch from measuring the *resistance* of lights on a light board to measuring *voltage* on a clip car's battery. Mr. S assured me, "Okay, you got the hard part out of the way, all that's left is the easy part." That made a big impression on me. He was able to easily quell any anxiety I had with a simple encouragement. *I thank him for that.*

Mr. S also served as my instructor for the Advanced Electronics course. During that lab final, he was gracious enough to show me where I could find each of the five sensors in my clip car's engine that I needed to identify. I had become so frazzled that I could not even find the numbers that were taped to each one for easy viewing.

Mr. V in Manual Trans helped me during the lab final when I had to use a dial gauge (I HATE those things!) to measure out-of-round in three places on a transmission shaft. As I mentioned in the Introduction, my problems with that device hark back to Basic Engines. He could see that the gauge kept slipping from the top of the shaft while I turned it. For whatever reason, I could not keep the spring-loaded plunger on top of the shaft while I turned it. The clock was ticking, with just a few seconds to spare before my time ran out. As Mr. V called out the last ten seconds, he actually slowed down the count, to let me finish on time: "*FFFFFFFFFIIIIIIIIVVVVVVEEEEEEE . . . FFFFFFOOOOOOUUUUUURRRR . . . TTTTTTTH- HHHHRRRRREEEEEEE . . . TTTTWWWWWOOOOO . . . OOOOOOOOOONNNNNNNNNNEEEEEEEEE.*" That final "one" must have lasted *at least* ten seconds. He paused while I wrote down the last number . . . and then he announced, "Time!" Mr. V then laughed uproariously and ambled over to me, grinning widely. "You just made it," he said, still laughing. I had to grin a little myself. *He is a good guy, Mr. V.*

One of my previously mentioned friends, Gordon, hails from out of state and was a competent tech prior to arriving at UTI. Despite his considerable skills, Gordon did not do so well in the lab finals for Mr. V's Manual Trans course because of a slight . . . miscommunication. One of our tasks for the lab final was to indicate the "ID" of a transmission bearing (in essence, a metal ring) on the table. "ID" is shorthand for "inner diameter." To complete the task, you need to use a T-gauge and a micrometer. The T-gauge is a small, spring-loaded device in the shape of a "T." There are different sizes for different components. The micrometer is a measuring device that looks like a small clamp in the shape of the letter "C," with a handle you twist to expand or contract the distance between the two ends of the "C." For this lab task, you place the T-gauge inside the round component, let it expand to fit the diameter, then turn the handle of the T-gauge to lock the tool. You then place the locked T-gauge inside the micrometer and turn the handle of the micrometer until both ends of the "C" close around and touch both ends of the T-gauge. The handle of the micrometer displays markings that can then be read to determine the length of the T-gauge, which will be the inner diameter of the component.

Gordon already knew how to perform this measurement, but when he saw "ID" on the lab final he thought it meant "Identification Number." So instead of measuring the inner diameter of the transmission bearing and entering a number like "1.613 inches" on his answer sheet, he found the component identification number which was stamped on it and he wrote something like "CA-1417632HJ19." He never even realized his mistake until the following day. Mr. V called us each into the lab, individually, to receive our lab final scores. Gordon later said that he immediately knew something was up because when he entered the lab Mr. V was already laughing hysterically. He said that Mr. V was laughing for at least thirty seconds and had to put his hand on Gordon's shoulder to steady himself from falling off his seat on the edge of the desk. Once Mr. V's convulsions finally dissipated, he delivered the bad news to Gordon, who—impressively—took it pretty calmly. Gordon sheepishly reported to us his *faux pas* upon his return to the classroom. We all broke out laughing ourselves. It was one of those moments when you "had to be there."

Another example of an instructor helping me out during the lab final was in my Electronics Diagnostics course. The lab final consisted of four different stations in the lab, with different measurements or questions to be answered at each station. I made it through the first two stations pretty easily, but the third station was my nemesis. At this station, we had to record certain information from the clip car's engine and a variety of its electrical components. The first task was to do a "cable to post voltage drop" of the battery to determine if there is an unwanted resistance (such as corrosion around the battery post and battery cable). However, my clip car had a battery with side posts—not the typical top posts—so I was unable to do this test. I put "N/A" on the answer sheet, which was the correct answer. *Ok. So far, so good.* The next step was to do a voltage drop (that is, determine the amount of voltage running through a component) of the car's charging circuit. To do this test, the car engine must be running. I turned on the engine, got out my DMM, and placed the positive and negative probes where I thought they should go. I heard the instructor, Mr. M, seated at his desk in the lab facing directly at me, begin to laugh loudly. I paused, wondering if perhaps he was laughing at me. I checked over my work . . . and suddenly realized that the reading on the DMM was not what it was supposed to be, so I moved the negative probe to the case of the alternator. *Voila!* I got the expected reading and wrote it down. The last task at this station was to use a diagnostic tool called a MicroVAT[30] to do a full-system test on the car's battery, starter system, and charging system. We had used the MicroVAT in our prior lab assignments, so I already knew how to conduct the test. However, I forgot to turn off the car's engine from the prior voltage drop test. In order to do a full-system test using a MicroVAT, the vehicle must be in park. All loads (e.g., lights, radio) must be off, the doors must be closed, and the key must not be in the ignition. *I fucked up.* The car was running, so the MicroVAT could not do a valid test. As I started running through the steps on the Micro-VAT, I kept getting error messages that indicated the components could not be tested. I redid the test several times and kept getting the same error messages. As I grew increasingly frustrated, I heard Mr. M laughing out loud again. He knew what I was doing was wrong, but he could not say anything since it was a test. I told Mr. M that I was getting error messages, thinking that maybe the MicroVAT was not working correctly. Mr. M asked me what the error message was. I told him, and he offered that perhaps there was an unnecessary load on the battery. I turned the lights on/off, I turned the air-conditioning on/off, I turned the radio on/off, but I could not figure out what the "load" was that was preventing the MicroVAT from starting the test. The clock was ticking, and I was now becoming really panicked. Finally, Mr. M walked by my clip car on his way to help another student. As he did so, he said, "You probably can't hear it, Mr. Ellis, because of all the noise in the lab—but it sounds like your engine is running." *That* was my clue. *The engine is running!* It is supposed to be off at the beginning of the test. I now knew what I had to do. But then Mr. M announced to the class, "Five minutes left in the test!" *Ouch! Why does this always happen to me?* I quickly turned off the car engine and started the full-system test, crossing my fingers that

---

30   A MicroVAT is a machine built by Snap-On that contains a battery, starting and charging system analyzer, a DMM, a cable voltage drop tester, and more.

I would finish on time. As it turns out, I did NOT finish on time. When Mr. M called, "Time!", I regretfully had to disconnect the MicroVAT from the engine. The MicroVAT was still in the process of printing out the test results on a lengthy roll of paper tape. I did not get a printout of the entire test. So, several points were deducted from my score because I did not record all of the test results. Mr. M gave me a big hint, for which I am grateful. Without his assistance, I'm fairly certain my lab final score would have been much lower.

I mention these examples to demonstrate that the UTI instructors often try in various ways to help students pass their courses. I am surely not the only student who struggles under the pressure of the timed lab final, and I think the instructors are very well aware that not everyone handles time pressure well. I suspect I was not the only one who received friendly comments or hints during the lab finals, either. These acts of kindness by the instructors showed that they know some students have a difficult time making it through classes and lab finals, and that sometimes they need a break. *I know I did.*

As I noted earlier, attendance is very important at UTI, as employers want to be certain that their hire from UTI will show up for work. Attendance is tracked very rigorously and, as I previously mentioned, if a student misses more than twelve hours of class during a course, he or she fails the course and must repeat. Taking attendance at the beginning of class is a critical part of this metric. As the year progressed and we entered the winter months, arriving at school on time became more and more of a challenge. The traffic on the major highway between my house and the UTI campus would become one giant parking lot during a heavy snow or heavy rain. I tried factoring in a time buffer during one of those bad weather days so I would not risk being late for class. The school was aware of potential delays due to inclement weather and would sometimes give a thirty-minute or longer grace period at the beginning of class, so that students caught in bad weather would not be docked attendance points for being late. School was in fact cancelled a number of times due to snow or icy conditions on the roadways. We experienced a "polar vortex" in early 2019 that caused the school to close for two days. The instructors, too, would sometimes use their discretion to give students extra time to make it to class—even if the school did not offer an official reprieve. My instructor for Advanced Diagnostics, Mr. N, did this several times. On bad weather days, he would occasionally announce at the start of class, "All right, because of the bad weather we will delay the start of class for fifteen minutes. While we are waiting for the others, you can use the time to call your loved ones to tell them you arrived safely." *Call your loved ones? Really?* I chuckled at that odd expression, but that was one of his signature phrases: "Call your loved ones."

I can recall when my instructor for Fuel and Ignition, Mr. G, cut a student a break on the last day of the class (the Friday when the 20-point final exam is given). The student had already missed twelve hours of class and thus was one infraction away from "houring out" and failing the course. The instructor, Mr. G, was well aware of this risk and mentioned it to this student in class the day before. His warning: "Don't be late tomorrow or you will hour out." He was good-natured about it, but still: rules are rules. The next morning, as the rest of us were filing in to class before the bell, we all noticed this particular student was not in class. His absence instantly became the hot topic of conversation. *Will he make it? Will he fail the class?* Mr. G, realizing the student's precarious position, asked one of the absentee's friends to call him and make sure he arrived before the bell. "He's on his way," the friend reported. The clock ticked down to the starting time. Eventually, the bell sounded. *The guy's a no-show.* We all held our collective breath. Mr. G walked up to the front of the class to take attendance, but before doing so, he first poked his head out the door. He looked up and down the hallway to see if the student was coming. I could tell that Mr. G really did not want to fail this guy. He announced to the class that he was going to give the student a break and read his name last, just to give him extra time. He then began reading aloud the names of the students in the class in alphabetical order. But unlike every other time he had taken attendance, this time he read the names *very . . . very . . . slowly*. We were all focused on what was going on now. Again, we were all chattering. *Will he make it? Will he fail?* About ten names in, Mr. G paused, walked over to his desk, read a few emails on his computer, took a long swig of coffee, looked at the door, then walked back to the center of the room to continue reading off the names. As he moved down the list, he kept poking his head out the door to check the hallway. Just before he got to the missing student's name, the student burst into the room. Mr. G told him, "We knew you were on your way, so we took our time with the attendance." I looked at the clock. The guy was clearly late: five minutes after the bell. "You *just* made it," said Mr. G. "Fuck, yeah!" responded the student, smiling, as he headed triumphantly to his seat. We all broke into applause and cheered.

CHAPTER 6

DIRTY WORK

When most people think of an auto mechanic, they typically envision a guy who toils under a car or over the fender of a car's engine, gets grease on his pants, has dirt smudged on his face, and whose hands are permanently black and grimy. An adult version of Dennis the Menace. Television and movies have contributed to this stereotype. Often, the first introduction the audience has to an auto mechanic in the story is a disembodied voice with feet sticking out from under a car or the mechanic wiping his dirty face with a rag from his back pocket, wearing the telltale oil-stained overalls and a battle-worn expression from a hard day's labor. In fact, a common term for an auto mechanic is "grease monkey." According to Wikipedia, "grease monkey" dates to at least 1928. The term may have originated during the Industrial Revolution in Great Britain, when children were used to grease the large rotating axles that transferred power from one centralized steam engine to all the machines on the factory floor. These children, covered in grease and crawling along tight spaces in the ceilings, were equated with monkeys.

Fixing cars and trucks *can* be a dirty job. But not every auto mechanic or auto technician (the terms are synonymous, although the preferred term these days is "auto technician") gets dirty every day working on cars. Not every maintenance or repair job requires someone to crawl under a car; stick his or her hands into an engine, transmission, or suspension that may be extremely dirty; or get sprayed with grease, oil, gasoline, coolant, battery acid, or brake fluid. Especially today, as more and more components of an automobile are electronic, the work done to maintain or repair an automobile or truck may not require the mechanic to get dirty at all. He or she might only be required to diagnose a check engine light with a scan tool (which involves nothing more than connecting to a port under the dashboard); replace a broken bulb, actuator, or electronic sensor; fix a loose electrical connection; or reprogram a computer module with new software. In other words, the work that goes on to maintain and repair automobiles and trucks can be no different from what an IT worker does to fix a broken computer. But that's not the image in most people's minds.

If you have not been to a car dealership lately, you might be surprised by how clean some of the service areas can be—not just the area where the customer sits to wait for his or her car, but the area where the techs actually do their work. Some of the auto manufacturers have pushed their dealers to create a modern, well-lit, organized, and open workspace for their techs. The German automobile manufacturers (Audi, BMW, Mercedes, Porsche, and VW) in the past few years have been pioneers in this regard. In one BMW dealership I visited recently, a massive picture window dominates one wall of the waiting area, allowing you to watch the techs work on cars. The service area is sleek, modern, and clean. The work space is filled with high-tech equipment and everything is color coded. The toolboxes in all the work bays are identical, giving a very polished presentation to the entire service area. Each of the techs wears a shop uniform with his or her name and the name of the BMW dealer printed clearly on the front. You would be hard pressed to call these techs "grease monkeys."

When techs do get dirty, the dirty part of working on cars is not just relegated to the engine or the underside of the car. Often, the interior of the car and the trunk are extremely messy and dirty, making it that much more difficult for the tech to do a repair. Both instructors and UTI students recalled horror stories about what they discovered when working on customers' cars—including rotting food, used baby diapers, smoking paraphernalia (both the legal and the illegal kind), and empty beer and liquor bottles. One instructor told us he once discovered a wad of one-hundred-dollar bills stashed inside the center console and another said he once found a loaded gun under the driver's seat. I suspect these stories are pretty common.

The area that seems to attract most of the filth and refuse is the trunk, which evidently many people use as their "mobile garbage can." Techs are never happy when they are forced to wade through a mountain of garbage in the trunk to access the spare tire or to open a panel that allows them to work under the car on the gas tank or fuel system or the mounting point for a suspension component. One UTI student told us about a customer who brought her car in for service at the dealership where he is a porter.

"She was very hot," he said. "*Very* hot. But when I got in her car to move it, I saw it was a fucking mess! It was filled with all kinds of shit, dirty laundry, and it smelled really bad. I couldn't believe it," he shuddered.

"*Eeewwwww*," agreed all the other students, in unison.

The automobile industry needs techs. While development continues on the production of an entirely autonomous, self-driving car, no one has yet made a car that can repair itself. Cars themselves are becoming more complicated. Every year there are more electronic components, more computers built into the car, more sensors, cameras, and safety devices, and more choices for fuel systems— gasoline, diesel, electric, hybrid engines, ethanol, methanol, liquid petroleum gas, and compressed natural gas. When I was telling friends and neighbors about my desire to retire from law and attend technical school so I could work on cars, more than one person shared with me that he used to work on cars but gave it up years ago. Once components shifted from mechanical to electronic, it became much more difficult to keep up with the new changes in repair procedures. I can certainly understand the reason for these comments. From my year at UTI, it was apparent to me that an effective technician needs to be trained in many disciplines. Each technician must be a mechanical engineer, an electrical engineer, a chemical engineer, a HVAC repair expert, a carpenter, an IT help desk person, and an environmental engineer. On top of that, every technician needs to be aware of the laws that apply to the repair of vehicles, the rules that apply to emissions, and EPA requirements. Today's technician must be well versed in the standards for repair and shop safety set by the auto manufacturer, the shop where he or she works, and the state/federal government.

According to the National Automobile Dealers Association (NADA), US technical colleges and training programs graduate about 37,000 service technicians each year. But retailers actually need about 76,000 new techs annually just to keep up with job creation and retirements and resignations.[31] And that shortage does not take into account the independent shops or other employers that also require techs, such as companies that maintain huge fleets of cars—so the demand for techs is even greater. According to UTI's latest annual report,

> The market for qualified service technicians is large and growing. In the most recent data available, the United States Department of Labor (US DOL) estimated that in 2016 there were

---

31   "NADA Foundation Launches Workforce Initiative Interactive Website for Aspiring Service Techs: The Auto Retail Industry is Facing a Critical Shortage of Service Technicians, Which Will Only Get Worse in the Coming Years if Not Addressed," NADA Press Release dated January 25, 2018.

approximately 749,900 employed automotive technicians in the United States, and this number was expected to increase by 6.1% from 2016 to 2026. Other 2016 estimates provided by the US DOL indicate that the number of technicians in the other industries we serve, including diesel, collision and motorcycle are expected to increase over this ten-year period by 9.2%, 8.5% and 0.3%, respectively. . . . As a result of these factors, the US DOL estimates that an average of approximately 125,200 new job openings will exist annually for new entrants from 2016 to 2026 in these fields, according to data we reviewed.[32]

By all accounts, therefore, there is a HUGE demand for technicians, both for auto (that is, gasoline engines) and diesel (that is, cars, trucks, and other vehicles that run on diesel engines). More jobs exist than there are people to fill them. The tech shortage is a constant in the industry. Publications such as *Automotive News* regularly report on the shortage.[33] The reasons for this shortfall are complicated. One possible explanation is that the economy is so good in the United States that people who would otherwise be attracted to the auto industry are finding well-paying jobs elsewhere. Indeed, one instructor at UTI informed me the last time large numbers of students enrolled in UTI was in 2008, when the Great Recession forced many employees who were laid off to seek retraining opportunities in other industries. Also, more and more senior technicians are retiring, in part because they are aging out of the industry. As you age, it is harder to work such a physically demanding job. And the industry is seeing more trained technicians become disillusioned with job prospects or

32 UTI Annual Report for the fiscal year ended September 30, 2018, filed on SEC Form 10-K on November 30, 2018, pages 5–6.

33 "AutoNation steps up to recruit more techs," *Automotive News*, July 1, 2019, p. 16.

working conditions—or both—and move to other technical industries that can use their skill sets but pay more.

The increase in the minimum wage in a number of states may also be a factor here. People who might otherwise consider a new career as a technician might be less likely to leave their current place of employment if their wages are rising under these new laws.

Another factor is the emphasis that society still places on attending a four-year college and getting a college degree before entering the workforce. Technical schools are not viewed by many families or high school guidance counselors as a first choice for graduating seniors. Instead, they are often seen as a last option. One of my friends at UTI, Gardetto, told me his high school guidance counselor was apoplectic when he told her that he wanted to enroll at UTI because he loved working on cars. Gardetto said he was an A student at his high school and had briefly considered attending a four-year college. His guidance counselor told him that he was "throwing his life away." "Why would you want to do that?" she chastised him. Gardetto had worked on his Subaru for years and had rebuilt the brakes and part of the engine and transmission, and had serviced the vehicle himself. He hung out with a group of friends who had cars and liked to work on them. Gardetto is extremely bright and eager to learn. We were in a number of courses together and would often informally quiz each other before tests. I have every confidence that Gardetto will be a great technician.

The UTI admissions person who assisted me confirmed that UTI has an uphill battle when it comes to convincing high school guidance counselors that technical school is an appropriate option for post-secondary education. UTI has an active effort underway to share its story as well as convey the opportunities it offers to new high school graduates who may not wish to attend (or who may not be able to afford) a four-year college. Several groups of high school guidance counselors toured the campus while I was attending UTI.

The administration gave them a hard sell, I have no doubt. During their visit, I happened to walk past a classroom where a group of high school guidance counselors watched a PowerPoint presentation on the school and the advantages of a technical education for certain students.

And yet, the efforts to address the tech shortage remain largely uncoordinated. Various groups or constituencies have efforts underway to attract more people to becoming technicians. The auto manufacturers, the car dealer groups, the NADA, UTI, and other technical schools are all trying to accomplish this same goal.[34] In January 2019, the NADA Foundation launched its Workforce Initiative to promote careers in the auto industry and provide a single source for would-be techs to identify training opportunities. Techforce Foundation, a 501(c)(3) charitable organization, provides scholarships and grants to men and women who want to train to work as technicians. All of these programs are independent of one another. No single organization or umbrella "owns" this issue, so their efforts naturally overlap and may even compete with one another for money and resources.

Not surprisingly, the ultimate driver for attracting new people to this industry, as well as an important element for retaining them, is money. It is why the students come to UTI in the first place. They want to make money. I came to UTI to learn, but the other students want to make as much money as they can, as quickly as they can.

The ability to make good money is a major selling point for UTI. During the open house I attended, compensation was a major point during the presentation by the senior admissions officer. He threw some numbers up on the screen as examples of what types of income techs could expect to earn, assuming a certain number of hours worked in a year. While I don't recall the exact numbers, the annual wages he showcased hovered around $60,000. One woman

---

34   *Id.*

asked him during the following Q&A session whether there really was a return on investment, given the significant cost of a UTI education. The admissions officer was extremely reassuring and confident that the money was there. In many of my courses, instructors often mentioned how being a good technician could translate into financial success. One instructor, Mr. O, owns a number of Harley Davidson motorcycles. Mr. S owns a lake house where he would go every weekend. Mr. N has a collection of pinball machines. Almost every instructor touted the financial rewards that awaited us as technicians after graduation.

And yet, as promising as the financial opportunities may seem for an aspiring technician, the reality is, in some cases, very different. Technicians are paid under a unique compensation system. It is not hourly pay or salaried pay. It is a flat rate or "book time" system, meaning they are paid at a flat rate for each job that they complete. Each job has a different flat rate, depending on the difficulty of the job as determined by the flat rate manual.[35] For example, let's say that the job is to replace the spark plugs in a six-cylinder engine and the flat rate for that job is two hours. Let's also say this tech has a few years of experience and his hourly rate is $26 per hour. Since the job has a flat rate of two hours, the tech will be paid for two hours of his time (total of $52), regardless of how many hours it takes him to do the work. If he is efficient and can do the job in just one hour, he still pockets the entire $52. If something happens that causes the job to take longer (e.g., one of the spark plugs is seized and won't come out or breaks off during extraction, causing extra work), he still gets paid $52, but does not get paid anything more for his extra time.

Recognize that the flat rate paid to the technician is not the same as the amount paid by the customer. For almost every job performed

---

35　The flat rate manual is usually published by the factory, at least for warranty work. Independent shops may also use Chilton's, Mitchell, or Motor publications for their rates.

by the technician, the customer is given a fee estimate up front that includes the shop's gross profit. So, in our example, the customer might be quoted $250 to replace the spark plugs. In that case, the gross profit to the shop is $198, less the shop's costs for any parts for the job. In some areas, labor rates charged to customers are approaching $200 per hour. So, you can see that the cost of the tech's time to perform the work is not a large percentage of the cost charged to the customer.

The flat rate system is the most popular system used by dealers and repair shops. It has advantages and disadvantages. It promotes productivity and efficiency, maximizes the shop's labor output, and protects the shop from paying labor costs during slack periods when there are few customers. The technician is paid only for the jobs he or she completes. On the other hand, because the technician is trying to "beat the book time" and finish the job quickly so he or she can move on to another job, it encourages risk-taking and shortcuts, and quality may suffer as a result. Should the customer return because the repair was not done correctly, the tech who did the initial work has to redo it. This situation is referred to as a "come back." No tech wants a "come back," and techs with few or no "come backs" are largely viewed as quality techs and are highly prized. And yet, if a tech slows down to make sure he or she does a quality job, that tech may not be able to beat the "book time" and thus will make less money.[36]

In order for a tech to be successful under a flat rate system, he or she must not only be fast and efficient at various car repairs, the shop must be one that is busy on a steady basis so there is always more work and another job to do. While there is little a tech can do to ensure a constant demand for business, he or she can focus on

---

36 Note the fewer jobs the tech completes, the less money the shop makes, since the shop's profit from the service department is geared to the number of jobs completed by each tech. Accordingly, both the tech and the shop have a vested interest in completing as many jobs as quickly as possible.

learning the skills necessary to become an efficient tech. The industry standard for techs is 1.5 flat rate hours for each hour worked in the shop. That means an experienced tech is expected to complete sixty hours of flat rate work for every forty-hour workweek. For a tech who is just starting out in the business, that sixty-hour target must be extremely daunting. It is a goal for the junior tech, but it may take a long time to achieve it. In addition, since techs are paid flat rate hours only for those jobs completed, it could be a number of years before a junior tech begins earning significant money. And because dealers and independent shops don't want to pay top dollar to techs who are just starting out in the business, flat rate at the beginning may be as low as $12–$14 per hour. This flat rate might be slightly higher in some union shops. Assuming a tech starting out is paid $14 per hour and achieves an average of thirty-five flat rate hours per week, that tech will earn over the course of a year a little less than $25,000. That is not big money, particularly if the tech has a family to support. And if the tech had to borrow money in order to pay for tuition at a technical school like UTI, that educational loan repayment will place a big burden on the family's budget.

If a tech can quickly learn to become more efficient and earn more flat rate hours for the week, then his or her pay will of course increase. And if a shop has a higher pay scale, then of course the opportunity to earn is greater for the aspiring tech. But make no mistake about it: very few dealers or independent shops will pay a lot of money to a junior tech who has little or no prior experience. Many service managers expect all new hires to start out at the bottom and work their way up the ladder. Entry-level jobs include lube techs, performing oil changes, and tire rotation. Lube techs are paid very little, and if there are no openings in the shop currently for technicians, it may be a few years before a new hire can advance. And "moving up" may not mean making that much more money, at least initially. I asked around and was told that the high end of the flat rate pay scale for auto techs is around $40 per hour. If you are efficient and can book a lot of flat rate hours at that rate, then, yes, you can make good money. For example, booking even forty flat rate hours per week at $40 per hour averages to around $80,000 per year. But again, this flat rate hourly pay is the top end of the scale and how long does it take for an aspiring tech to get to this level?

There is some anecdotal evidence that UTI students may get better paying opportunities for their first job out of school due to the established reputation of the school. However, financial success ultimately depends on whether the tech possesses basic skills and the ability to learn quickly on the job so he or she can advance and receive a higher amount per hour of flat rate time. The higher the flat rate amount, the more money a tech can make. My instructor in my Automatic Transmissions course, Mr. M, prided himself on having the highest flat rate hours for many months in the shop where he had once worked. In his shop, there was an endless supply of work. He told us he once set a record of over eighty flat rate hours in one week. Other instructors told us of certain work, such as recall work (where the manufacturer, not the customer, pays the bill), which could be very lucrative for a tech under a flat rate pay system. If there is an easy fix for the recall, such as a part swap or a software update, and the tech can do several cars at once, the tech can amass a lot of flat rate hours in one day. One of my instructors, Mr. S, is a staunch defender of the flat rate system. He said that under the flat rate system, you can make more money without working more hours. I would generally agree with that statement, but with the caveat that you are first a smart and efficient technician.

There are some notable exceptions to this compensation system. A few dealers have moved away from the flat rate system for their techs. They use other compensation approaches, including an hourly rate regardless of the hours worked, a bonus system for hours booked

over a certain minimum, and other types of incentive arrangements.[37]
The vast majority of shops still use the flat rate system, however, so
flat rate compensation will likely remain a staple of the industry for
a long time.

I worry for the young people starting out as techs who are blissfully unaware of the financial challenges they face in this industry.
Even if they receive scholarship money to help pay for their education, it is unlikely to cover 100% of their tuition. So many will
likely have a school loan to repay, a burden that will follow them
post-graduation. And while the best and the brightest at UTI go on
to prestigious manufacturer-specific programs, like Porsche or BMW,
that provide post-graduate training along with the potential of dealership jobs at the conclusion of training, most UTI graduates do not
follow this roadmap. Most UTI graduates have the simple goal to
find a tech job after graduation and go from there. While even the
Porsche and BMW students must work up the ladder at their dealerships to get the big bucks, they are starting off from a better position
because the manufacturer has provided them additional specialized
training and thus has an investment in their success. I suspect these
lucky few get more support in the early stages of their career than
most other UTI students.

Another financial burden that automotive techs must bear is the
cost of tools. I was surprised to learn that techs use their own tools
when they repair cars at dealerships and independent shops. Certainly,
the bigger tools such as the alignment rack, the tire balancer, the lift,

---

37   Because demand for techs in the diesel industry is so high, many shops
specializing in truck and diesel engines have moved away from a flat rate
compensation system in order to attract more technicians. My fellow UTI
students who were specializing in the diesel field told me they had lots of
job offers that paid them on an hourly basis, not a flat rate system—with a
signing bonus and tool allowance in some cases, as well. Diesel jobs are thus
higher-paying jobs than automotive jobs at the moment.

etc. belong to the shop. But the impact wrench, sockets, wrenches, oil filter wrench, screw drivers, torque wrench, breaker bar, pry bar, tire gauge, etc. used by the tech to repair your car belong to the tech. Once hired, the tech brings his or her own toolbox to the shop and uses these tools to work on your car. When the tech terminates employment, the tools leave with the tech and go on to the next job.

This fact is noteworthy because the cost of tools is considerable. Not all tools are expensive, but many of them are pricey. It could put a tech back several thousands of dollars just to have the basic tools necessary to work in a shop. Over the years, an experienced tech may acquire a variety of specialty tools as the need arises. Indeed, some tool companies like Snap-On and MAC Tools have representatives in tool trucks who visit repair shops on a regular basis to sell the techs more tools. More than one instructor informed us that he had over $100,000 worth of tools in his possession, a vast collection amassed over years in the industry. I can attest to the high cost of tools. As my education at UTI progressed, I felt empowered to purchase some basic tools for myself. It is an expensive proposition to acquire tools, even tools that are not brand name. The toolboxes themselves can be expensive. Not only that, but there are plenty of cool, shiny tools for sale that scream, "Buy me!", making it hard to resist the temptation to buy them.

Another aspect of the auto industry I learned during my year at UTI is the interesting dynamic that exists between technicians and customers. Instructors often shared stories about previous customers and their cars. A consistent theme in these stories is the preponderance of customers who are "idiots," "crazy," or "out to lunch." A common refrain from the instructors is that most customers don't know anything about how cars work, are suspicious of technicians who they expect will financially gouge them, or are "know-it-alls" who tell the technician what work needs to be done on their car. Perhaps the most common customer depiction I heard from my instructors was the customer who assumes that merely by plugging in a scan tool to the port under the dash, the tech can determine exactly what is wrong with the car and how to fix it. I have no doubt that these stories we heard from the instructors are true. And I am embarrassed to admit that I myself have acted like one of those "crazy" customers at some point in my life.

In my Professional Service Writing course, we learned customer relations skills from an instructor who spent many years working with customers in a dealership. The idea behind this course was to prepare us for dealing with all types of customers (including customers like me) we are likely to encounter. Our instructor, Mr. M, taught us that customers communicate in one of four ways: (1) they ask for routine service; (2) they describe a problem that has a simple solution (e.g., a broken headlight that needs to be repaired); (3) they diagnose their own problems and ask for a service or repair that they "think" will solve it; and (4) they ask you to diagnose the problem. This list may be an oversimplification of the various ways that customers communicate when they bring in their cars for service, but it is a good start for helping future techs understand that not every customer communicates in the same manner. One big takeaway for me was when Mr. M mentioned that many customers who bring their cars in for service are already unhappy. They are often upset that something is broken on their car, mad that they have to take time off from work, annoyed that they have to wait several minutes before talking to a service advisor,[38] and vexed that they have to pay money for the work done on their car. Mr. M was once a service manager at a dealership (the top service position in the store). He provided us with valuable lessons, honed by his years of experience, on how to deal with customers who are "bent out of shape" because they have to bring their cars in for service. He

---

38   The service advisor used to be called a "professional service writer," hence the name of the course.

described one customer who was so upset, he could see the man's fists were balled up as if he was ready to punch someone out.

I am happy to say Mr. M was not describing me, as I never balled up my fists when talking to a service advisor. But, yes, I have been plenty upset in the past when I had to bring my car in for service and had to take time away from the office. I expect I am not alone in this regard. I recall once raising my voice at a service advisor who told me that my one-year-old Audi S4 needed a four-wheel alignment (not covered by warranty) that was going to cost me $189. How could that be possible? I babied that car and drove it very carefully, even to the point of driving around minor potholes. *A wheel alignment?* I was in a rage, as if it was a personal affront. I was spitting mad. Yes, that was me to a tee (P.S. The service advisor graciously agreed to do the wheel alignment for free). In hindsight, I can see what an ass I had been.

As I mentioned above, a customer may be suspicious of the dealership's intentions, suspicious that the work does not need to be done, or suspicious that the price for the work will be too high. During my Professional Service Writing course, we discussed the role of the service advisor. The service advisor is supposed to be the first contact and port of call—a buffer, if you will—for the customer. The system is in fact designed to insulate the technicians from customers. If the customer has a question, the service advisor answers it (or may get the technician to help answer it). The system usually works smoothly. Where it breaks down, of course, is if the service advisor does not know what he or she is talking about, cannot answer the customer's questions, or becomes defensive when the customer challenges whether the work needs to be done, etc.

It also breaks down when the service advisor suggests additional work that the customer may not have requested. Service advisors make a commission on work they recommend that is not the original reason why the car was brought in for service. This practice is referred to as "upselling." Upselling is very common, not only in dealerships, but also in independent shops. Often, the additional work that is suggested does not really have to be done. Some of it may simply be preventive maintenance. Or some of it may be work that will have to be done at some point, *so why not do it now as long as the car is in the shop?* In our course, we were encouraged to engage in upselling (in shops where there is no "service advisor," the technician may actually have customer-facing communications). We were told not to sell work that is unnecessary, but to think in terms of what the customer is likely to need down the road anyway. *So, why not suggest an oil change now, even though it has only been a few months since the last one?*

I understand why the industry promotes upselling. The automotive repair industry needs to keep busy, so why not try to sell more repair work? But in my own experience, I have noticed that service advisors are increasingly pushy when it comes to recommending additional repairs. A friend of mine recently emailed me a printout he received from his service advisor. They "highly recommended" $800 worth of work on his two-year-old car. I compared the recommendations with the owner's manual for the car and my UTI reference materials. I determined that none of the work was necessary. In particular, one recommendation was to flush the automatic transmission fluid, but the car has a monitor light on the dash that illuminates when the computer says it is time to flush the A/T fluid. The warning light had not come on and the car had not accumulated the level of mileage at which the owner's manual said the work is likely needed to be done. *So why do it now?* In my own case, I took my car to a dealer to remove a wheel lock that was stripped. I had tried on my own to get it off but was unsuccessful. The service advisor prepared a repair order for the wheel lock removal but also informed me I needed new front brakes (both pads and rotors). When I asked him why, he could not answer the question—other than to say that it was based upon mileage. As the majority of my mileage on this car is highway miles and both the pads and rotors were in great condition with lots of meat left (I checked), I politely told him no. Another customer who might not know what to look for, however, might have said yes just because the service advisor suggested it. This aggressiveness is causing customers to be increasingly suspicious that much of the "recommended" work does not actually have to be done. And in turn, it is giving service departments a bad name and fostering mistrust between the automotive repair industry and customers. As a result, more customers and potential customers are extremely skeptical whenever they receive "recommendations" for unsolicited work to be done to their car.

I think few UTI students have themselves been customers at a dealership. As a result, they view customers at arm's length. Customers are foreigners. They are outsiders. They don't know what we, as technicians, know. They did not attend technical school, as we did. As a result, many UTI students exhibit a superiority complex over customers, if only because, as technicians, these students are better trained in how cars work than most customers. But this attitude generates an *"us vs. them"* dynamic that I found to be a little unsettling. Because I was first a customer before embarking on my training as a technician, I can identify with all the emotions and concerns customers often have when bringing a car in for service. During the Professional Service Writing course, I felt like I was straddling the Great Divide. I am both a customer and a technician. I understand the perspectives of both sides, so I could never side with one over the other.

Some (although not all) of the UTI instructors contribute to this *"us vs. them"* dynamic by telling stories that emphasize their superior technical knowledge and their ability to decipher the customer's concern—particularly translating strange noises into a concrete diagnosis and repair. The anecdotes about customers trying to replicate unusual noises in a car are pretty funny, and the instructors have told them so often they have gotten it down to a *shtick*. In addition, we heard plenty of horror stories of customers who did not take care of their cars, who drove for days with a "check engine" light illuminated on the dash or a low-tire-pressure warning displayed, or who were unschooled in the most basic maintenance of the car. The stories about customers who are dumb or naïve were a little less funny to me, if only because I consider myself to be naïve and I am sure I've said something equally dumb to a service advisor at some point in my life. Mr. M in Basic Engines shared an anecdote about an elderly woman, driving an older car, who complained about the engine hesitating and stumbling whenever she drove it. When he went out on a test drive with her, he discovered she had mistaken the choke (found on an older car, which restricts the flow of air, thereby enriching the air-fuel mixture while starting the engine) *for a purse holder*. She had the choke pulled out all the way from the dash (with her purse hanging on it) as she drove the car around town. No wonder the engine did not perform well! Most automobiles today do not have a manual choke like the car in this story, but the message about communication and understanding the customer's concern remains relevant.

Another chestnut is the one about the customer who complained that the wheels on one side of the car were going at a different speed than the wheels on the other side of the car. When the technician could not replicate the customer's concern, the customer went out on a test drive with the tech and pointed to the speedometer and the tachometer located side-by-side on the dash. The customer incorrectly assumed that both dials were speedometers, one for the left side and one for the right side. Since the speedometer (which shows the speed of the car, in *miles per hour*) and the tachometer (which shows have fast the engine is turning, in *revolutions per minute*) are two different indicators and are rarely at the same clock position on the dash, the customer assumed there was something wrong with the car's wheels. The tech then had to spend some time educating the customer on the two gauges and what each one measures. I have heard this story more than once from several different sources, and part of me thinks it is an urban myth. In any event, I can safely proclaim that I was never as naïve as that particular customer.

Despite the *"us vs. them"* dynamic, customers are a necessary part of the process. Without customers, there would be no cars to fix or work to perform. In our Professional Service Writing course, we were told, "The customer, not the employer, pays the wages," further emphasizing this point. Technicians can be *better* technicians if they empathize with customers, rather than poke fun at them. The horror stories and "urban myths" shared at UTI also reinforce the notion that technicians are different from most customers because of the techs' considerable training and knowledge. Technicians can and should take pride in the skills they have learned to diagnose and repair automobiles. I take no issue with the team-building aspects of sharing these funny anecdotes about customers and their cars. If it creates a sense of camaraderie among techs, then that is a good thing. But customers should not be demonized or viewed suspiciously or pigeonholed into simplistic categories of behavior. Perhaps I am overreacting to what I heard at UTI because I was a customer before I was a student. But what I wish is that every technician who works on my car views it as my prized possession and cares about fixing it and fixing it right (the first time) as much as I do. More than one UTI instructor delivered this same message to the class, simplified as, "Take the same amount of care fixing the customer's car as you would your own car." Unfortunately, given the questionable condition of the cars that some UTI students drive, I am not sure that message resonates as soundly as it was intended. *Just saying.*

CHAPTER 7

"SO, WHAT DID YOU LEARN TODAY?"

Since I started UTI knowing precious little about cars and how they work, every day at school was a gift. I learned something new every day. It did not matter if the day was spent in lab or in the classroom. It did not matter which one of the seventeen courses I was taking. I was soaking up everything like a sponge. Whenever I could, I took copious, detailed notes. When I did not understand something, I asked a question or did some internet research on my own after class. I often did both. My sources of information included the lectures, the course materials, my notes, and the big red Course Book that contained our self-study chapters. Occasionally, one of my classmates explained something to me and I learned from that. It was a rich time. And while it merely lasted one year, I could see myself easily continuing onward.

My goal to "decipher the black box" was emphatically met by UTI's Automotive Technology program. In all of our courses, we were taught the names of different components and what they did, the systems with which they were associated, and what might occur if one or more of the components were faulty. After a year of memorization, I am now pretty good at opening up the hood of an engine[39] and identifying the parts of the engine that lie underneath. I can tell what is related to the ignition system, the charging system, what lines carry fuel, the air intake manifold, the exhaust manifold, the A/C system (including the high side [high pressure – hot] and the low side [low pressure – cold]) lines, the water pump (which pumps a mixture of water and coolant throughout the engine block and the radiator), the ABS[40] system, the PCV[41], the EGR[42] valve, and so forth.

I also know how to perform research using AllData, Mitchell's, and other information services that provide technical information about each make and model of automobile sourced directly from the automobile manufacturers. UTI has subscriptions to these services so students are able to research a lot of "how to" information, diagrams, step procedures for the testing, replacing, and repairing of components, and even suggested labor times for determining how to charge for the work. In almost every course, we looked up information on a computer so we could get comfortable with using a computer and searching these databases of information. I found out a lot of information is NOT readily available through a simple Google search or watching YouTube automotive videos. And I have seen plenty of YouTube videos that have provided inaccurate or incomplete explanations of how to repair certain components. *Caveat emptor.*

For me, the year was filled with plenty of "lightbulb" or "a-ha"

---

39   Believe it or not, simply opening up the hood of a car can be a technical operation that requires explicit directions. For some cars it is not intuitive where the hood latch is or how to release it. I recall a Lincoln Navigator in one course that had me stumped for several minutes. When I could not figure it out, a friend in my lab group had to demonstrate how to open the hood.

40   Anti-lock braking system

41   Positive crankcase ventilation

42   Exhaust gas recirculation

moments. One of them occurred in my Automatic Transmissions course when Mr. M explained how a torque converter (TC) works. A TC gets the car moving from a dead stop, as well as allowing the car to stop and idle in gear. It transfers the rotation of the crankshaft to the input shaft of the transmission through the use of hydraulic fluid. *That's right: fluid gets the car moving from a dead stop.* I think that is nothing short of amazing! As the crankshaft of the engine turns, it causes a pump or impeller to throw fluid forward towards the engine and a wheel, called a "turbine." As the fluid hits the turbine, the vanes of the turbine force the turbine to turn and throw the fluid back in the direction of the pump towards a small wheel called a "stator." The stator can move in only one direction. It is locked onto a shaft, and the turning of the stator from the fluid thrown at it by the turbine ultimately causes the transmission to turn and drive the wheels of the car. It is like a system of water wheels with torque multiplication. I still shake my head in amazement at the notion that the movement of fluid causes a car weighing thousands of pounds to move from a dead stop.

Since there are so many electronic components, sensors, relays, and computers in cars nowadays, it is no surprise that a great deal of emphasis in the Automotive Technology program is on electronics. There are three courses dedicated to electronics, and electronics are discussed as part of the curriculum in almost all other courses. We learned during the open house I attended about UTI's emphasis on electronics, and in fact we sat through a sample "class" in which the instructor explained to us Ohm's law. For those of you who don't remember this one, Ohm's law is "E = I x R," in which "E" means volts, "I" means amps, and "R" means resistance. *Sound familiar?* We were given small lightboards to play with so we could get a demonstration of how Ohm's law is applied to an electronic circuit. Included in the list of items we had to bring to school as new students was a set of colored pencils (used to draw wiring diagrams, color-coding the various circuits). Electronics is a critical part of UTI's program.

I am a bit of a geek when it comes to science. I loved my science classes in high school and did very well in them. I think my love of science helped push me in the direction of tax law when I was a lawyer, as the approach to tax law can become almost scientific in its application. Accordingly, I was thrilled at the prospect of diving into automotive electronics. I cannot say the same for the other UTI students, as most of my friends were nervous about taking these courses. There were plenty of stories of students who failed these courses and had to retake them. Several friends of mine from Basic Engines did fail one or more of their electronics courses. The UTI instructors and the more senior UTI students made it sound like the courses were incredibly difficult. For me, I saw it as another challenge.

I had a blast in my electronics courses at UTI, and while I did not earn SOC in any of them (my friend Rogers was SOC in two of them), I learned a great deal. One of the reasons I learned so much was the teaching style of my instructor, Mr. S. He was my instructor for two of the three courses: Electronic Fundamentals and Electronic Technology. Mr. S is gregarious and outgoing, with many years of experience working for Audi. He had a great approach to teaching. He expected everyone to follow the UTI rules regarding uniform, attendance, and professionalism ("No f-bombs!"), but he also enjoyed joking around and giving people a chance to relax a little. If he had a funny anecdote, he encouraged others to share one as well. During our lab assignments, many of which consisted of working on light boards in the classroom, Mr. S would play rock music (including Steely Dan!) through the classroom speakers so we had some musical accompaniment as we worked. No other instructor did that. I thought it lightened the mood and made for a more relaxed atmosphere. We even sang along with the songs. In one demonstration, Mr. S showed us the proper way to solder two wires together. To demonstrate the strength of the solder, he had another student (who was a pretty big guy) try to pull the wires apart in a tug-of-war with Mr. S. Both Mr. S and the student volunteer grunted and groaned, and much to our amusement, were unable to pull the wires apart. Point made, and it was fun to watch the action.

But more importantly, Mr. S did two things that enhanced the learning process for us. First, he presented to us *his* version of basic electronics, distilled from his years working in the field. He told us that he found the official course materials to be confusing. He said that he and one of the other Basic Electronics instructors had agreed that a different take on the material might be easier for students to comprehend. To make sure we learned the basics, he handed each of us a notebook he had made that consisted of about thirty lined pages stapled together. He told us to take notes using this notebook, which we all did. He also wrote on the whiteboard (and made us copy) massive amounts of information regarding basic electronics. We covered the parts of an atom: the proton, neutron, and electron. He taught us what voltage, amperage, and resistance were. We covered conductors, insulators, magnetism, the difference between a series circuit and a parallel circuit, and various ways to test for voltage, amperage, and resistance in a circuit. I cannot tell you how helpful this method of presenting the information was for me, and for a lot of the other students. This notebook became a reference source of information for other courses as well. I referred to this notebook in several other courses to supplement or reinforce the new information I learned. I heard more than one student claim he would use the notebook in the field and keep it in his toolbox at work. In comparison to the material on electronics in our red Course Book, the information we wrote in our notebook was much easier to understand.

The other teaching enhancement Mr. S employed in Electronic Fundamentals was to spend time at the beginning of class formally reviewing the material we had covered the prior day and had written in our notebooks. He would ask a question out loud, and the entire class would provide the answer in unison. For example, he taught us that voltage is defined as the force needed to push or pull an electron out of orbit from an atom. It is electrical pressure.

He would ask us, *"What is voltage?"*

We would respond, *"The force needed to push or pull an electron out of orbit from an atom. It is electrical pressure."*

This review format took five to ten minutes each morning. Mr. S remarked that repeating these basic rules out loud as a group was a learning technique taught in the army. I was never in the army, but this approach worked for me. While I am a pretty good note-taker, writing down something does not necessarily make me learn it. It helps, but it is not bulletproof. On the other hand, repeating something in class, day after day, was a really effective way to learn. Little catch phrases we often repeated, like "When voltage goes up, amperage goes up," stick in my brain to this day. It proved to be a powerful teaching tool.

Rogers and I were in the same lab group for both electronics courses with Mr. S. We shared the same intellectual curiosity about the subject, and we would often quiz each other before tests to make sure we had learned the material. Sometimes I would review my notes and if they did not make sense, Rogers was someone I could ask for clarification. He was a smart kid. Rogers was as steady as a rock during the lab finals and almost always got a perfect score, regardless of the course. In the Electronic Fundamentals course, I missed getting a perfect score on the lab final because I incorrectly answered one question: "What do you do if the battery has surface discharge?" The correct answer is to clean the battery. I was not thinking straight during the lab final and said the answer was to replace the battery. Wrong. *Oh well.*

The school schedules the Electronic Technology course right after the completion of Electronic Fundamentals. All of us who passed

Electronic Fundamentals thus continued the following Monday into Electronic Technology, coincidentally also taught by Mr. S. In this course, we learned the more advanced (and in my opinion, more interesting) aspects of the electronic automotive world, including how to use scan tools and oscilloscopes to test electronic sensors and actuators. Sensors are inputs to the car's computers, which provide information on speed, pressure, light, temperature, and position. Sensors are located all over the car and the information they "sense" is relayed back to one or more computers to be analyzed. Actuators are outputs of the computer. They are devices that receive an electronic signal from the computer to do something. They control different components and systems of the engine, such as timing of the engine, fuel adjustments, emissions, climate controls, and the suspension. We learned about alternators (which charge the battery) and ignition systems (which provide spark to ignite the air/fuel mixture in all of the engine's cylinders). We learned the names and types of different electronic sensors in the engine, such as crankshaft position sensors, camshaft position sensors, O_2 sensors, mass air flow sensors, manifold absolute pressure sensors, knock sensors, engine coolant temperature sensors, and intake air temperature sensors—to name a few. We also learned whether the sensors generate analog or digital voltage signals, under what conditions the sensors generate a low voltage signal or a high voltage signal to the computer, how many wires each sensor has (helps for visual identification), what sensors work best for a particular application, what actuators are triggered when the car's computer reads these signals, how to connect an oscilloscope to the sensors to view the waveform they are supposed to generate under normal operation, and how to test whether the sensors are operating correctly.

In this course, we were also introduced to the various computers installed in a typical automobile. Today's cars have a multitude of computers in them, including the power train control module (PCM), which controls all power train components such as the

engine, transmission, and differential; the anti-lock brake module
(ABS), which controls brake application; the ignition control module,
which controls ignition spark and timing of that spark; the traction
control module, which manages the car's controls for wheel slip; the
body control module (BCM), which controls all internal and external
accessories on the car; the suspension control module, which controls
the ride, stiffness, shock absorbers, and strut action; and the engine
control module, which controls all the sensors and actuators of the
engine. We learned that the computers "talk" to each other over net-
works in order to share information. For example, the vehicle speed
sensor (measuring how fast the car is going) provides an input signal
to the ABS module. The ABS module, in turn, shares the vehicle
speed information with the PCM (which needs the data for the
purpose of activating cruise control, for example). The PCM shares
the information with the BCM, which in turn shares the information
with the door lock modules (in order to lock the doors once the car
reaches a certain speed). In this way, each computer that requires
the vehicle speed data gets the same piece of data generated by the
vehicle speed sensor. As you can tell, this course provided me with a
ton of new, highly technical information to digest. The car geek in me
was very happy. This course entailed a lot of memorization. Unlike
in Electronic Fundamentals, however, we did not recite in class the
information we needed to learn. In Electronic Technology, we were
on our own.

One of my favorite lab assignments in Electronic Technology
was where each lab group had to diagnose a fault in a car's electrical
system to determine what was causing the fault. For this exercise,
we were in the classroom and each lab group worked at a training
board with various switches, sensors, relays, and actuators built onto
the board. Mr. S would secretly throw a switch behind the board to
create a fault. Our job was to diagnose why a component did not
work. *Was it an "open" (that is, a break in the electrical circuit) in the*

*wiring, in a relay, or in the component itself? Was it a "short to ground,"
causing a fuse to blow? A "short to power," causing a component to turn
on unintentionally?* Each lab group had to figure out on their own
each of the faults and determine what was causing them. This lab
assignment took place over a two-day period. Rogers and I were in
the same lab group and were able to figure out a number of the faults
pretty quickly. As a result, we would get "emissaries" from other lab
groups who would ask us what we found. Mr. S was pretty loose and
allowed the lab groups to exchange information. He simply wanted
to ensure that no lab group copied the final write-up from another
group. Our group did pretty well and ultimately solved all but one
fault, which stumped the entire class. Rogers was the steady hand in
our lab group, devising a "process of elimination" approach for this
lab assignment. I enjoyed this lab because it simulated real world
problem-solving that, as technicians, we would encounter in the field.

Other than the electronics-related courses, the other group of
courses I found most interesting were two related courses focusing
on fuel, ignition systems, driveability, and emissions. The driveability
concept is probably new to you. It certainly was to me. For these pur-
poses, "driveability" refers to how well the engine runs. A driveability
problem could include one or more of the following:

the engine will not crank or cranks slowly;

the engine won't start even though it has normal cranking speed;

the engine stalls, runs rough, misfires, or hesitates;

the engine runs hot;

there is a lack of power;

there is spark knock;

there is backfire from the exhaust or air induction system;

the engine runs on after you turn it off ("diesels");

the engine gets poor fuel economy;

there is smoke coming from the exhaust, which appears white,
black, or blue;

there is an odor coming from the exhaust;

and so on . . . [43]

In order to make a proper diagnosis of any of these problems, the technician must have a firm understanding of how the fuel, ignition, air induction, exhaust, and emissions systems are supposed to work on an engine. That is why driveability is covered in tandem with the topics of fuel, ignition systems, and emissions. In fact, in many cases, driveability problems are caused by incorrect settings or faults in the fuel, ignition, and emissions systems. These topics are therefore at the heart of the Automotive Technology program. Diagnosing and solving driveability problems can be some of the most challenging for an automotive technician, we learned. These problems also can be among the most common in the field as well.

During these two courses, we learned about fuel control. The PCM is the computer that controls the fuel system in a car. The PCM is programmed to provide the optimum engine performance, fuel economy, and emissions for which the car was designed. This technology is not new. Using a computer to regulate the fuel system in a car dates back to the late 1960s. An engine needs to have the proper air/fuel mixture to run correctly. It is expressed as a ratio of air to fuel. The most desirable A/F ratio is 14.7:1, meaning 14.7 parts air to 1 part fuel. When the engine does not have enough air, or has too much fuel, the A/F ratio is called "rich." An example of a rich ratio is 9:1. A rich ratio is not good for a car's engine, as it can cause excessive carbon buildup in the combustion chamber from the excess fuel that cannot be burned during combustion. In the event there is too much air, or too little fuel, the A/F ratio is called "lean." An example of a lean ratio is 20:1. Lean ratios can cause a surge at cruising speeds. They also burn hotter and can cause excessive engine wear. The PCM

---

43 *Advanced Diagnostic Systems*, ADTA-126, Student Guide, Chapter 5, "Driveability Diagnosis", pp. 5-3 and 5-4 © UTI (2011- 2015).

is constantly monitoring and correcting the A/F ratio. With the right scan tool, you can see the car's current A/F ratio. Some cars have a dedicated gauge that shows the driver the A/F ratio. The data point is a common one for those who race cars or modify engines, but even a typical driver can see what it is. Assessing the A/F ratio is a continual learning process for the PCM, and varies depending on the driver's driving habits and the environmental conditions (e.g., outside temperature, altitude, and so forth). This monitoring process has a name. It is called "fuel trim." We studied fuel trim in these courses covering driveability, and as a result I was able to diagnose and solve a problem I was having with my own car. Allow me to explain further.

There are two different types of fuel trim, both of which can be read using a scan tool on a car. One is called "short-term fuel trim" (STFT) and the other is called "long-term fuel trim" (LTFT). STFT is a short-term correction, usually a result of a glitch like a sticking valve or an intermittently stuck fuel injector. LTFT is a long-term correction to the A/F ratio and is the one used in diagnosis, as it provides a view of the engine's history over a longer period of time. LTFT is expressed as a percentage and is either negative or positive. If the percentage is a negative number, the PCM has been *taking away* fuel from the A/F mixture for a long time because the engine has been running *rich* (too much fuel in the mixture). If the percentage is a *positive* number, the PCM has been *adding* fuel to the A/F mixture for a long time because the engine has been running *lean* (too much air in the mixture).

Still with me? In my case, I have a 2000 Mustang. My car's check engine light (CEL) came on, so I had to diagnose the problem. I plugged in a scan tool to the port under the dash to find out which diagnostic trouble code I had. The code was P0305, which is a misfire in cylinder 5 (the car has eight cylinders). The technical information I found suggested the most likely culprit was either a bad spark plug, a bad fuel injector, or a bad ignition coil. I confirmed my preliminary diagnosis with Mr. V (my instructor from Manual Trans, who is also a Ford instructor), and he agreed that one of these components was probably the cause of the misfire. None of those components was faulty, however, so none of them were causing the misfire. The car has very low miles on it, so I would have been surprised if one of those components had failed, but you never know. I did happen to notice on the scan tool, however, that my LTFT was "+15%." As described above, that high, positive LTFT number indicated that the PCM was over the long term *adding fuel*. Why would the PCM do that? Likely because I had a *lean* fuel mixture problem caused by either too little fuel or too much air, and the PCM was trying to correct for it. I talked to a tech friend of mine who specializes in Mustangs, and he mentioned that the stock air intake on my particular car has a common problem. The intake is made of plastic and is prone to cracks, resulting in an air leak. A leak in the air intake manifold could cause too much air to go into the combustion chamber, resulting in a lean A/F mixture *for which the PCM would add fuel like crazy to compensate.* We took off the air intake manifold to inspect it and . . . *Voila!* There *was* a crack in it. A small one, but a crack, nonetheless. We installed a newer, stronger air intake manifold from Ford Performance and . . . *Guess what?* Problem solved! The LTFT immediately went down to 0–1%, which is within the normal range.

More importantly, the CEL has not come on since we installed the new air intake manifold. I think that the lean A/F ratio caused by the crack in the old air intake manifold must have been severe enough to cause a lean misfire in cylinder number 5. It is possible for a car engine to misfire if there is too much air in the A/F ratio. *I'm getting carried away, but if it isn't obvious, I find all that goes on "under the hood" of a car to be pretty cool!* And it is a perfect example of what I learned in school and why the car is no longer a "black box" for me.

Too often, if a part fails on a car, the proposed fix is to replace the bad component with a new one. However, merely replacing a bad spark plug, coil, or fuel injector, for example, may not fix the underlying issue that caused the component to "go bad" in the first place. Manufacturers are steadily improving the level of quality in car components. Cars these days generally last a lot longer than they had in the past. A few decades ago, a car that had 75,000 miles on the odometer was considered an old car in need of a lot of maintenance. Today, a car that has 75,000 miles on the odometer is just a "teenager." Many cars are built to last 150,000 to 200,000—or more—miles, provided regular maintenance is done on the car. Our instructors warned us not to just throw new parts at a problem, hoping that would solve it. If the underlying problem is not addressed, then the customer will be back in the shop again with the same problem and whatever goodwill you might have established with that customer will be lost. As a result, much of the curriculum at UTI focuses on teaching students how systems are supposed to operate, so we will have a head start in diagnosing why a particular component failed.

One of my favorite lab assignments during the entire year took place during one of these driveability courses. The name of the lab was "Turnover – No Start" or "TONS," for short. In this lab assignment, each group was assigned a clip car where the engine would turn over, but not start. Each car was bugged by the instructor to not start. It was our task to diagnose the problem and identify what was going wrong. TONS is an apt name for this lab assignment because it was *tons of fun*. Our instructor, Mr. O, invented a backstory for each car so we had a little information to begin our diagnosis. But for the most part, we had to cycle through each of the various systems on the car: fuel, ignition, emissions, and so forth, in order to diagnose the no-start condition. We had all the tools in the lab at our disposal, as well as our DMMs, and we were allowed to access the computer to get wiring diagrams of the car's engine provided by the manufacturer. No two cars had the same bug, however, so it did not help us to ask another lab group what they found on their clip car.

Our first clip car was a 2003 Toyota Corolla. The backstory that Mr. O invented was that the car had not started ever since it was serviced by another shop. The owner was so mad at the other shop that he'd brought it to "our shop" to see if we could figure out what had happened. My lab group progressed through the car methodically and found a loose battery terminal. We reattached the battery terminal and tried to start the engine. *No luck.* The fix could not be that easy. We next checked for power and ground in the ignition coils. Guess what? There was power, but we could not confirm a ground for the coils. *Why weren't the coils grounded the way they were supposed to be?* The wiring diagram proved very helpful here, as we were able to locate two ground wires on the engine. But they were all attached. *What gives?* We poked our heads into, around, and under the engine to look for another ground wire. Ultimately, one guy in our lab group, lying on his back on the floor under the engine, found it. It was hidden by the firewall. We had missed it on the wiring diagram. It was loose, completely disconnected from its mounting point on the engine. We connected it to the valve cover, as referenced in the manual, and the engine started instantly.

The other clip car we diagnosed was a 2002 Ford Focus. The backstory Mr. O invented was that an elderly woman had parked her car while on a quick run to the store to buy food for dinner. When she emerged from the store, the car would not start. Her car had worked fine when she drove it to the store. The car was towed into the dealer, where we had to figure out what had happened. This one was proving to be too difficult for us. We checked for power, ground, and spark, and everything passed the test—but we still could not get the car to start. We did find, however, that there was no fuel pressure, meaning that fuel was not getting to the engine. *Why was that?* We checked the fuel pump relay but that was not the culprit. It was working correctly. We were stumped. Ultimately, Mr. O offered us a big clue. He added that the car was bumped in the parking lot while the woman was in the store. One guy in our lab group owned an older Ford like this one and was able to figure out the problem. It was the inertia fuel shutoff switch, a device found in many Ford vehicles, which shuts off the fuel automatically when the car is in an accident in order to prevent a fire. It is, essentially, a safety device. In this case, however, the IFSS can be triggered if the car is bumped very hard near the area of the car where the switch is located (usually in the rear quarter panel on either side or at the back of the car). So even though the invented story featured no *major* accident (just a parking lot bump-and-run), the car would not start. *Case solved!* We found the IFSS (the clip car had no trunk, so the IFSS was wired into the car under the carpet near the back behind the passenger seat), reset the switch, and the engine turned over right away.

The TONS lab assignment, like many of the labs we were assigned over the course of the program, taught us to diagnose problems effectively. Diagnosis is a process. In some cases, there is an easy fix, but in other cases the technician must go through a step-by-step process of elimination to determine the cause of the problem. It helps, of course, if the same problem has occurred before on the same model of car. As more than one instructor noted, there are lots and lots of possible reasons why something does not work on a car or why a car has a driveability problem. There are potentially hundreds of possible explanations. However, the key is to not think of all of the *possible* causes. The key is to determine a list of *probable* causes. If you understand the system in the car and how it should function correctly, you can often limit your search to a short list of *probable* causes fairly quickly. And that's what makes a good technician a good technician.

CHAPTER 8

MY OLD SCHOOL

Around the middle of my Automotive Technology program, I started to grow weary. Despite learning so much, I was feeling the effects of half a year's worth of school: Seventeen courses, seventeen lab finals, and seventeen 20-point final exams in total. *Could I really do it?* Even though I was halfway through the program, it seemed like it would be forever before I would graduate. I sensed that the rest of my friends felt the same way as the year progressed. And many of these students faced an even longer road to graduation, especially if they planned to continue their education with manufacture-specific training that involved an additional twelve, fifteen—or more—weeks of classes. When I met up with my friends in the hallway, there was less chitchat, more solemn expressions and more talk of how tired they were—how much they hated their part-time jobs, their room-mates, or their current instructor. You could see that the enthusiasm and energy we had during our Basic Engines course had waned. In some cases, instead of stopping in the hallway to chat, they would simply briefly make eye contact as they walked by (as if to silently say, "What's up, Ellis?"). I sensed many of them were turning into auto tech zombies. *Not good.* But I understood what they were going through. Although I had an easier time of it than they did, I, too, felt the strain of the long slog to the finish line. I tried to stay focused but it felt harder and harder to keep up the pace.

People dropped out of school along the way. Some houred out of a course or failed a course and never returned to school. We never heard what happened to those students. Westbrook, for example, the funny guy who was a little older and gave dating advice to the younger guys, never finished the program. He houred out of two courses in a row and never came back. We suspect he was counseled by the school to take some time off so he could determine whether he really wanted to go through the entire program. The school does not like to give "course breaks" on a regular basis unless there is a serious financial, health, or other (e.g., military service) need.

As the year progressed, my friends from Basic Engines and other students with whom I took classes recognized that I was an A student and often approached me with questions or requests to explain things to them. Sometimes it would occur during a break, when the students were looking over the self-study chapter in the Course Book in advance of a test. Sometimes they wanted to copy my notes. I did not mind sharing my notes at all, but my handwriting is pretty bad (as a result of my bad thumb on my writing hand) so there were plenty of times both the other student and I were scratching our heads to determine what the heck I had written in my notes. I enjoyed explaining things to other students. It helped me confirm my understanding as well. And every now and then I had something wrong or backwards, and it was only because another student had asked *me* a question that I was able to sort things out. I recall more than once, another student would say, "Ellis, you should be an instructor at UTI." I was flattered, but I knew that would never happen. To be a UTI instructor, you have to have considerable experience in the field—which I don't have. That would always be my standard response. Perhaps they sensed that my ability to explain something combined with my balding head made me "instructor material." I knew this was not the case.

And as the year progressed, I became more confident about my own car repair abilities and more willing to take things apart and try to fix them. Towards the end of the program, I decided I knew enough to be able to replace an old fuel filter in my 2000 Mustang. The fuel filter is located under the car near the gas tank at the back. Not a big deal, as I had the special tool to do the job and I could put the car up on jack stands. So one weekend, I decided to try my hand at this minor repair. I did some research on AllData and determined how I was supposed to relieve the gas pressure in the line (the car is fuel-injected) before working on the fuel filter. But of course, there were . . . *uh* . . . some "challenges" for me (nothing is ever easy, is it?), and I ended up getting gasoline all over my clothes. But I got the rear of the car up on jack stands, got the job done, and replaced the fuel filter. I spent the rest of the weekend patting myself on the back and thought I had a great story about my successful repair to share with my friend, Alonzo, the following Monday. He and I were in the same course together and sat next to each other.

On Monday, Alonzo comes into class, sits down, and says, "'Sup, Ellis?" He then proceeds to tell me that on the previous Friday, as he was driving home from work, the transmission in his Pontiac blew up. He showed me a picture of a gaping hole in the transmission and trans fluid all over the street. "So what did you do?" I asked. He told me he sourced a replacement transmission from a local junkyard, removed his old transmission and the engine in one piece using an engine hoist, installed the new transmission, replaced some old seals and other parts he saw needed replacing, and with the help of a friend, put the new transmission and old engine back into the car. He connected everything back together and road tested the transmission to make sure it worked properly. Oh! And he took videos of every step of the process as well. "Took me about nine hours, start to finish, but the car now runs better than it did before," he said. "I drove it to school this morning, no problem." I was stunned. I just sat there in amazement of his weekend repair story and his talent. I did not know what to say. I decided not to share my "great repair story" with him. How could it possibly compare to *that*? And Alonzo is only nineteen.[44]

A year of school is still a year of school. It is a long time, regardless of what you are doing. The schedule never changed. It was the same every day: Wake up at 4:15 AM, leave the house at 5:00 AM, drive to school, start class at 6:30 AM, first break, lunch, end of class at 12:45 PM, drive home, eat lunch, study, eat dinner, go to bed. As the year progressed, I started to ease up. I was doing pretty well academically, with a number of SOCs under my belt and a 4.0 grade point average. I still took notes in class, but not as many. I studied only the night before an exam, rather than daily. I started to guess what questions would be on each test, just for fun.

My test-taking skills were pretty good. I always said that in a multiple-choice exam, you have the right answer on the page—you just need to identify which one it is. My typical score on a 10-point test was a 9 or a 10, and if I really did not know the answer, I could usually narrow it down to two possibilities. At first, I used to beat myself up over the questions I missed. I used these mistakes as learning opportunities, though. And if I did not understand why the right answer was the right answer, I made sure to ask the instructor or look it up in the course materials afterwards. In the latter half of the program, I cared less and less if I missed a question, as more often than not I got it wrong because I either did not know the answer and had to guess or I read too much into the question. My

44 Alonzo snagged a coveted position in BMW's STEP program after UTI. "STEP" stands for "Service Technician Education Program." BMW pays for the training in exchange for a commitment to work in a BMW dealership. Many UTI students compete for these types of manufacturer-paid advanced training programs, but not everyone gets one because of the GPA requirements (e.g., minimum of 3.75 GPA) and because there are not that many positions available.

background and my training as a lawyer really did not help me much. More often than not, if I spent too much time analyzing the question, I overthought it and ended up getting the wrong answer. Some instructors actually told me that I was overthinking things from time to time, whether it was working through a test question or asking about something in class—or asking the instructor to explain how he wanted us to complete a lab sheet. I can see their point, since as a lawyer my training is to think about all of the different "what if" scenarios on behalf of a client. But when it comes to test taking in an automotive technology program, simpler is better. I was always looking for the "trick" question, but there never was a "trick" question on the 10-point tests. I can also say that, with a few exceptions, my first guess at an answer was the correct one. If I decided to change my answer after thinking it over some more, I usually got it wrong. "Go with your gut," is how I explain it to people. "Go with your first answer."

Here is an example. In my Brakes course, we learned that when building ABS systems, manufacturers can use either single stage solenoid valves (which have a single function to do) or dual stage solenoid valves (which have two functions to do). The test question was a "Tech A – Tech B" question, which is a common form of presenting a test question at UTI. The question said that two technicians were discussing valves in an ABS system. Tech A said that a single stage solenoid valve is used. Tech B said that a dual stage solenoid valve is used. Who is right? The choices for answers were:

A – Tech A is correct.

B – Tech B is correct.

C – Both Techs are correct.

D – Neither Tech is correct.

The correct answer is C. And that was what I initially put down on my answer sheet. But after I had finished all the questions and had reviewed my answers, I thought more about this question and decided that the answer should be D because I thought that Tech A was saying that *only* single stage solenoid valves can be used, and that Tech B was saying that *only* dual stage solenoid valves can be used. But the word "only" is not actually in the question, is it? I assumed it was implied in the question; that is, I read too much into the question. This is a perfect example of my "thinking too much." *I wish I could take that one back.*

I have always considered myself pretty self-aware, so when I got a test question wrong because I overthought it, on the next test I redoubled my efforts to not try so hard, to go with my gut, and to put down the first answer I thought was correct. Interestingly enough, over the last couple of courses, I found I did better on tests and scored a lot of 10s with this new strategy. Whenever I was in doubt, I just went with my first answer and turned in my test before I could overthink things. When it came to lab finals, however, I really did not have any strategy for dealing with my trials and tribulations. I wanted to do well on the lab final because doing so was the first step in getting SOC honors. The student with the highest lab score and a class test score of at least 90% is awarded SOC. I decided that getting SOC was not such a bad thing, and I thought maybe it would bring me some kind of honor at graduation (it did, as it turns out). So doing well on the lab final became my goal for each of my last few courses.

Truth be told, regardless of how poorly I thought I did on lab finals, I usually ended up with a pretty good score. Perhaps it is my nature to assume the worst, but in at least two situations (in addition to the one mentioned in the Introduction), I went home thinking I had completely blown the lab final. When I returned to school the next day, I found out that not only had I gotten a pretty good score, I'd gotten the highest lab score and SOC for the course as well. This 180-degree turnaround occurred in my Automatic Transmissions course and my Advanced Diagnostics course. The Auto Trans course is the one that Mr. M referred to as a "GPA-buster." I teamed up with my friend, Gordon, from Basic Engines, for our lab assign-ments, and we cruised through the disassembly and reassembly of an automatic transmission without any glitches. The lab final for this course consisted of two parts over two days. On day one, we had to answer written and multiple-choice questions. That part was worth ten points. I thought I did pretty well on that part. On day two, we had to go into the lab to do component ID ("ID" in this case means "identification") and take measurements using various testing tools. The day two test was timed (thirty minutes) and consisted of ten questions, worth two points each. Some questions were straightfor-ward, such as, "Which of the labelled components on your table is used for adjusting end play on a transmission shaft?" You had to know the answer and also recognize which one of the items on the table was that component. I did struggle with this particular question. I knew the name of the component, but I could not remember what it looked like. *Which one is it? Which one is it?* That one threw me for a loop. I made a wild guess.

The lab final questions that made me the most panicked and most frustrated were the measurements. *Again*, the measurements! In one case, we were asked to measure the turning torque on one shaft of the transmission. To make the measurement, you had to attach an inch-pound torque wrench to the end of the shaft, spin the shaft, and record the reading on the torque wrench. *Simple, right?* Wrong. *No inch-pound torque wrench was on the table. Yikes! How am I going to make this measurement?* I tried not to panic . . . but I panicked. I looked around at the others working away at their tables, and I could not see anyone else using an inch-pound torque wrench. I thought maybe there was an alternative way to measure it. Finally, I just decided to move on and answer the other questions in the time remaining, but my stomach was in knots and I was not happy. The next measurement we needed to make was to determine whether there was continu-ity (presence of a path for current flow) on each position of the transmission range switch on a transmission that was next to our lab table. To do this test correctly, you needed to remember how to turn the transmission range switch so that you would start in "Park," then proceed through the rest of the gears (Reverse—Neutral—Drive—Third—Second—First) and mark down your answers on the answer sheet. For whatever reason, I tried to do the test on the wrong switch on the transmission. I think it was the park-neutral position switch, and I ended up with a lot of "O's" (for "open" or "no continuity") when I should have had a few "C's" (for "continuity") instead. I ran through the test two times before I realized *I was testing the wrong switch* for continuity. I moved over to the transmission range switch, measured all of the positions and put down my answers. But I was so shaken by my mistake that I did the measurements twice, just to be sure. Precious minutes were wasted doing that one section of the lab final. By the time I was done, I had two minutes left in the lab final and one more question to answer (not including the measurement of turning torque—*Where the hell was the inch-pound torque wrench?*) When time was called, I predictably had not yet completed the lab final. I had gotten only halfway through the last question, so I left a few blanks. I did not have time even to review my answers to the other questions. After time was called, I tried to at least quickly look things over. The other students had already left the lab when Mr. M came over to me and said, "Mr. Ellis, I need your test *now*." I took a wild guess at the turning torque measurement, wrote it down, and handed Mr. M the answer sheet. As I was leaving the lab, I saw on his desk a pile of inch-pound torque wrenches.

"Oh, so that's where they are," I said.

"Of course," said Mr. M. "That's where we always keep them. I said in my instructions that any special tools you need for the lab final would be on my desk."

I slunk away, nursing my wounds. When I got back to the class-room, I quizzed Gordon. "Did you have to measure turning torque?"

I asked him. He said no. Evidently, each student had a different set of ten tasks to do for the lab final.

"How did you do?" I asked Gordon.

"I think I did pretty well," he responded. "And you?"

"I think I blew it," I said. "I think I really blew it." I was not a happy camper.

That night I told my wife about my travails on the lab final. I kept saying, "I think I really blew it."

Her response? "Don't worry so much. You probably did better than you think."

Turned out she was right! The next day we were told our lab final scores. We were called into the lab, one by one, so we could see our answer sheet, see our score and what we got wrong, and ask Mr. M any questions we had. I ended up with a 26 out of 30 on the lab final, which—all things considered—was outstanding for me. I had missed only two questions on the lab final: (1) The turning torque, for which I had guessed twelve inch-pounds when the correct answer was twenty inch-pounds, and (2) the very last question, during which I had run out of time and left a few blanks. The other answers I put down were all correct—including my wild guess at the component ID. The night before I had played out the "worst case" scenario in my head and thought that if I could get at least a 20 on the lab final, I would be fine. *But a 26!* I was pretty pumped. I mentioned to Mr. M how much I'd enjoyed his course and that I had learned a lot. We chatted for a bit about school and the class, and then he and I walked together back to the classroom so he could call another student into the lab. As we were walking down the hallway, he mentioned to me that I had earned SOC for the course. *I . . . was . . . stunned.* After all that panic and worry! I did not know what to say. But I said thank you and went back to my seat in the classroom. I was all smiles when I told my wife later that night what had happened.

In my Advanced Diagnostics course, the lab final consisted of three stations, each one timed for ten minutes. At the first station, we had to diagnose some readings from a hypothetical four-gas analyzer (which analyzes the gasses that are emitted from a car's tailpipe) to identify whether the engine was running rich, lean, or normal, whether there was a misfire, or whether there was false air. I had no trouble with that one. The second station was to connect a scan tool to the port under the dash in a clip car, record some of the data from the various sensors monitoring the engine, and then make a diagnosis of whether the sensors were operating correctly, how the engine was running, and so forth. The instructor, Mr. N, had "bugged" the car with a defect, and we were supposed to identify which sensor was defective by the reading on the scan tool. Here, too, I did not have any trouble. For the last station, we were required to hook up an oscilloscope to the "breakout box" for a clip car to record the electronic waveform that a particular sensor makes while the engine is running. We also had to label and identify on our answer sheet certain additional information such as the volts, time, trigger, and slope of the waveform, and whether the waveform was AC or DC. For this station, I was assigned to the Toyota Corolla and the sensor I had to measure was the mass air flow ("MAF") sensor. I knew from an earlier lab assignment in the course that I needed to set the scope to "10 volts" on the vertical axis and "5 seconds" on the horizontal axis in order to capture the waveform. I turned on the car, put my scope leads in the appropriate places in the breakout box, and then . . . *nothing*. No waveform. *Uh-oh*, I thought. *What is wrong?* I checked the scope. I turned the scope on and off. I turned the car off and back on, checked the leads, checked the lead placement, nothing. *Nada*. No waveform. *Here we go again*, I thought. *If I don't get a waveform and copy it down on my answer sheet, I will get a zero for this part of the lab final.* I looked around. Everyone else seemed to be doing fine. I could hear Mr. N chatting away with one of the other students who had finished his station already. I could hear Mr. N say,

"Five more minutes." Then, "Two more minutes." Then, "One more minute." I was completely stymied. I did not know what to do. So I made something up. I drew a grid pattern the way I thought it should look. I labelled the divisions and attempted to answer as many questions as I could without drawing a waveform. Finally Mr. N called, "Time. Please hand in your answer sheets." I had no choice. I decided I would make a wild guess. I drew a waveform that started above zero, rose up gradually, stayed at about 4.8 volts for a few divisions, then sharply came down like the edge of a cliff. I threw in a trigger point of about 2.2 volts, marked an "X" on the upward slope where 2.2 volts would occur, and handed in my answer sheet.

When I returned to the classroom, my friends asked me, "How'd you do?"

"I blew it," I said. "I really blew it."

I did not tell them I failed to get a waveform on my scope. I was too embarrassed by what had just happened. A few of them nodded knowingly as if to say, "Yeah, me too." I could not believe I was unable to get a waveform during the lab final. *What the hell happened?*

What happened, I later figured out, was that I was supposed to snap the engine throttle lightly to generate the MAF waveform on the scope. Just letting the engine idle would not do it. And I found this answer in my notes from the instructions that Mr. N gave us previously. He had told us, "For the Toyota, you may need to tickle the throttle to get a MAF waveform." *I should have known.*

The next day, we got our progress reports with our lab final score. When my name was called, I walked up to Mr. N's desk to get my report. I scanned the report as I was walking back to my seat and literally stopped dead in my tracks when I saw the lab final score: perfect 30. It was unreal. I could not believe how lucky I was. And yes, much to my surprise, I earned SOC for this course, too.

After I had finished nine of my courses, I was past the halfway point in my program, so I looked at the rest of my courses as a glide path to the finish line. I even made myself a written list of the remaining courses with a checkbox after the name of each course. As I finished one course, I checked the box to show I was done. Eight courses to go, then seven, and so forth. I could see I was making progress towards graduation.

My final course in the Automotive Technology program was Professional Applications. This course is a hodgepodge of different topics, although most of them are electronic in nature. The course covers electronic transmission controls, electronic suspension controls, ABS, airbags, low-emissions and electric vehicles, and GPS. Kind of an odd mix, but the variety of topics certainly made the course interesting. Two other students were also graduating after this course: Grossman, the veteran who had served in the Army, worked as a state corrections officer, and wanted a new career, and my friend Rogers. All three of us sat together in the front row, right in front of the desk where the instructor, Mr. S, sat. Over the course of three weeks, we had a chance to chat with Mr. S a bit during breaks and when there was downtime. That was a real plus, as we were able to get to know him. He is one of the more senior instructors at our campus, so he had a lot of great experiences to share with us.

During your last course at UTI, your schedule for the final week is somewhat abbreviated. First of all, you do not go to class that final Friday, unlike students who are not yet slated for graduation. Instead, you take your last 20-point final exam at 7:00 AM on Friday morning in the Resource Center, along with students from all of the other courses who are also graduating. The tests are graded on the spot, so a few minutes after you have taken the test, you know whether or not you are going to graduate. Graduation is at 1:00 PM that last Friday. Since you do not go to class that Friday morning, you must finish all of your lab assignments by the end of the day on Thursday. In Pro Apps, that meant that Grossman, Rogers, and I had to do our lab final and complete four other lab assignments (which were each relatively short, but still time-consuming) on the final Thursday. And if that was not enough, we were also required to take the last 10-point test on electric vehicles on that same Thursday, as all tests had to be taken and scored before Friday morning. Normally that would not be a big deal, but Mr. S had not yet completed the lecture on electric vehicles when we took the test. That meant we had to take our last test somewhat unprepared.

By now, you know me. I will save you the "Sturm und Drang"[45] of the lab final. Let's just say it was another example of "not my finest moment." It was a timed test that involved, among other things, recording a movie on a scan tool of the electronic operation of the car's transmission through all four forward gears. The key to success was being able to hold the transmission in each gear for forty frames so you could record on the scan tool the operation of the various sensors and solenoids related to the transmission. Each "frame" is one moment in time when the scan tool captures information from each of the car's sensors; it is a fraction of a second. My car proved "difficult" for me. I ended up not getting the forty frames per gear, but Mr. S, who has probably seen this before, knew I was trying and gave me credit for what little I could do. My scan tool kept shutting off and rebooting as I tried to record the movie. There was a loose connection where the scan tool plugged into the port under the dash, probably from years of use/abuse. Although visions of the lab final from Electronic Diagnostics (where I forgot to turn off the car before starting the full-system test on the MicroVAT) flashed across my mind, in this case it *was* the scan tool and its connection, and not me. Mr. S was very patient with me and came over several times to get it set up. Finally, he got it working by wedging the scan tool in between the spokes of the steering wheel so movement of the data cable would not be a factor. Again, another example of an instructor getting me

---

45   German for "storm and stress."

through the lab final. Mr. S gave us our scores on the spot. I ended up with a 26 out of 30, and I was *ecstatic*. Grossman got forty frames per gear, but, as it turns out, he forgot to answer some questions on the lab final, so I am not sure how he did. Rogers most likely got a perfect score on his lab final, as he usually did. I never did ask him about his lab final score, but I'm pretty certain he was able to get forty frames per gear for his movie.

Mr. S insisted that our lab group, that is, all three of us prospective graduates, be the first group to take the lab final. He knew we faced a heavy schedule that Thursday to get everything done by the end of class. By 8:30 AM, we were done with the lab final and I breathed a huge sigh of relief. I knew at that point I was going to graduate. The rest of the day was a blur for me. I recall for one lab assignment we went into the Resource Center to research some technical information and write it down. *More pencil whipping.* I think I had to sharpen my pencil three times because of all the writing. For the next lab assignment we had to use a GPS device to walk around the school's parking lot and jot down what we found at various GPS coordinates. Grossman, the veteran (he was once a drill instructor), said "I got this" and took charge of us walking around the parking lot to get the information we needed for our last lab sheet. At 12:15 PM, another instructor scooped us up and took us to another classroom to take our last 10-point test, the one covering a lecture that Mr. S had not yet completed. I think I guessed on three or four of the ten questions. I had studied a little for the test, but usually the lecture is where the instructor drops big clues about what material will be tested. Since Mr. S had not given us the entire lecture yet, I was "flying blind" and had no choice but to guess. As I had done very well up to that last test, I really was not too worried. I just needed a few more points on this test to get the minimum 70 needed to pass the course.

Once I was done, I purposely waited until Grossman and Rogers had finished their tests and left the room. I wanted to be the last one to turn in my test and go out the door, in part because I wanted to savor the moment. I knew I was going to graduate. This was not an issue. So I just sat there for a couple of minutes and took it all in. I thought about all I had been through, from that first day in Basic Engines all the way through today. I thought of all of the students I had met, the different instructors, the 4:15 AM wake-up, the daily commute to school, the long winter, all the studying, the tests, and those FUCKING LAB FINALS. I am sure the test instructor must have wondered why I was taking so long. Remember, these tests are not timed, so I was in no hurry.

It was too much to think about, as it turns out. I was, to be honest, a bit emotional. I felt the tears well up but I did not want to cry in front of this guy. *Why was I getting so emotional?* I was emotional for several reasons. First was simple relief from the stress of going the distance and finishing. I felt like I had just run a marathon of sorts. When I'd started, I was cocky. I thought it would be easy, and then it turned out to be harder than I thought. I had not missed a day of class. I studied hard, took tons of notes, and worried so much during the year about those times during my lab finals when I thought, *I blew it.* I ultimately did not blow it. Second, I think I was pretty proud of myself and of what I had been able to prove: a guy with no prior experience or background in automotive technology jumped into the deep end of the pool. I was so happy! And third, I was already starting to miss the place: the camaraderie, the feeling of being "one of the guys" (despite my age and background), and the routine that taught me so much and had been my anchor for the past year. I was sad to leave.

Luckily for me, the instructor was not even looking at me as I sat there and dabbed at my eyes. He was engrossed in a book. I got up, turned in my test, thanked the instructor, and left the classroom for the last time.

CHAPTER 9

THE LAST DAY

The next morning at 7:00 AM, I took my last UTI test along with forty-five other graduating students. In addition to Rogers and Grossman, there were other students I recognized from my other courses. After a few minutes of some overly complicated instructions and test mishandling (one student did not get a test and another student got two tests), we were all administered our respective 20-point final tests. Then we all waited as a group until our names were called so we could find out our scores. All three of us (Grossman, Rogers, and me) had already attained the minimum 70 in class points for our Professional Applications course before we took this last 20-point test, so we knew we were all going to graduate. It was just a matter of what our final class score would be. Once our scores came back, we were released. It was a little before 8:00 AM when I left the Resource Center, so I had a couple of hours to kill. Our instructions were to show up in cap and gown for formal pictures at noon. The graduation ceremony started promptly at 1:00 PM.

Graduation at UTI takes place every three weeks, as UTI also has a new entering class start every three weeks. So on the last Friday of every three-week course, the same day that many UTI students take their 20-point final test for whatever course they are taking, a group of UTI students graduates at 1:00 PM. The ceremony is relatively short. Mine lasted forty-five minutes, start to finish. When we marched into the auditorium in our caps and gowns to "Pomp and Circumstance," I noticed that the place was packed. My wife and daughter were in the crowd, on the aisle, and cheered as I walked by. They had gotten there early to make sure they had good seats close to the front. My wife later confided in me that she was sure that other parents who saw her must have assumed that her "son" was graduating from UTI. The speeches were short and poignant. The director of the school gave a speech. The head of the employment department gave a speech. Rogers was chosen to give a speech because he was valedictorian, not only because he had a 4.0 grade point average, but also because he had earned more SOCs than anyone else in the graduating class. In his speech, he mentioned how lucky he was as a UTI student—not only because he was book smart, but because he had a good roommate who motivated him to study, quizzed him in preparation for tests, and encouraged him to be successful in his pursuit of his education. I knew he was talking about Gordon, my friend who'd figured out how to defeat the monitoring device his parents had installed on his car in high school. An instructor, Mr. C, gave a speech encouraging us to keep learning even after school was over, stay safe, and give back by teaching others and sharing the knowledge and good work habits we learned at UTI. After that, we walked across the stage one by one to receive our diplomas and pose for photos with the head of the school. Once we had all walked across the stage and returned to our seats, the entire room watched a slideshow consisting of some posed and some action shots taken of UTI students at the school. Many of the pictures were of the backs of people's heads. A few photos were of students who were not graduating. It did not matter. It was a slideshow showing our friends and families the UTI classrooms and labs and students in action. Following the slideshow, the head of the education department had us stand up as a group. He said, "Graduates of UTI, you may now move your tassel from the passenger side of your cap to the driver's side." The audience laughed and the ceremony was over.

That was it: short, sweet, and to the point. Graduates scattered after the ceremony. I knew that some of them were starting long road trips. Grossman headed back home with his family. Rogers headed back as well. I had a chance to visit a little with Rogers' father and mother after the ceremony. I told them they must be very proud of their son. And they certainly were.

Three weeks later, I returned to UTI to watch my friend Alonzo graduate. Although we started together in Basic Engines, he'd taken a voluntary course break around Christmas so he could spend more time with his family. That meant he graduated three weeks later, within the next course cycle. His graduation was exactly the same as mine: same format, same speeches, same rhythm, and same finish. I wanted to chat with him briefly after the ceremony to wish him well. He was going off to Arizona to the BMW STEP Program, so I wanted to make sure I said goodbye to him before he took off. Surprisingly, Alonzo was very emotional about graduating. He was teary-eyed and he spoke very little. I could tell that graduation was very important to him and that he was feeling very proud of his accomplishment. I remembered the feeling I'd had three weeks earlier, after I finished my very last test and tried to soak it all in. I suspect he was feeling the exact same thing. I tried to talk to his mother and father, but their English was somewhat limited, making our exchange brief. I could sense, however, that they, too, were extremely proud of what their son had accomplished.

After leaving Alonzo, I looked around for another friend, Oduye, who I had noticed from the ceremony program was also graduating that same day. He is originally from Nigeria and recently moved to this country. I saw him in the auditorium during the ceremony, but after talking to Alonzo I could not find him. Oduye is a good guy who was in a couple of my courses and was also in my lab group for Brakes. He had originally started UTI in 2015, but had to stop because his family could no longer afford for him to go to school. So he took some time off, earned some additional money, and then returned to UTI to finish his education.

But I could not find him, so I headed out to the parking lot. On my way out, I ran into an instructor, Mr. P, whom I knew because he'd taught a course in the classroom next to mine several months earlier. I got to know him because, as an early riser, I was usually waiting at the door of my classroom for my instructor to arrive and unlock it. Mr. P, also an early riser, would often unlock the door for me so I could at least sit in the classroom rather than wait in the hallway. So he knew who I was even though he never taught me.

Mr. P noticed I was in street clothes, rather than in UTI uniform, and asked, "So, what brings you back to UTI? The graduation?"

"Yes," I said, "I came back to cheer for one of my friends today."

We had a chance to chat a little. I remembered at that time that I had heard a rumor about Mr. P, so I figured, *What the heck? Now is as good as any time to ask him about it.* So I did.

I said, "Mr. P, is it true that you have been in only three car accidents in your life, and in each case you were rear-ended by a UTI student?"

He laughed. "Yes, sadly, it's true." He then explained that at the old UTI campus, there was an intersection near the school at the bottom of a hill and, each time, he'd been rear-ended by a UTI student who was running late to class and drove down the hill too fast to stop in time. He then abruptly changed the subject.

"You know they want me to retire," he said. He just blurted it out, but I understood. Mr. P had suffered a mild heart attack last year and, after taking some time off, he had recently returned to teaching. "But I don't want to retire," he said. "I like what I'm doing, and I think it is important."

I responded, "I know what you're talking about, Mr. P. You're talking about giving back."

"That's right," Mr. P affirmed.

With that, we said our goodbyes and parted ways. Mr. P is not alone in this sentiment. I suspect that there are plenty of other UTI instructors who feel the same way as Mr. P. *They are giving back.*

I finally made my way to the parking lot and witnessed a lot of celebrating going on as graduates and their families started getting into their cars to leave the campus. The same thing had happened after my graduation three weeks earlier. I had to wait a few minutes for one group of students and families to pull out of their parking spots before I could move my car, and I am glad I did. Out of the corner of my eye I spotted Oduye, dressed in colorful Nigerian garb, getting into his car to leave the campus. I ran over to his car and knocked on his window.

"I'm glad I found you," I said. "I was hoping to see you graduate. Congratulations, Oduye!"

"Thanks, Ellis," he said. "I thought that was you getting into your car from across the lot. I remembered your car."

We chatted for a few minutes about the future and where we were headed. He mentioned he had one or two promising job prospects. I said to him, "I am so proud of you, considering everything you had to go through. You started school, took time off, and then came back to school to finish. You know, that is really inspirational, and I know how hard it has been for you. Great job!"

"And you, too," said Oduye. "You know you have been an inspiration to us, too."

"What do you mean?" I asked, a little surprised.

Said Oduye, "We knew how old you are, Ellis, that you were once a lawyer, and that you quit your job to follow your passion. *That* was inspirational for us, too. We said, 'If the old man can do it, so can we.'"

Wow. I was not expecting that one. *If the old man can do it, so can we.* So age was a factor after all. Well I'll be darned.

If the old man can do it, so can we. Well, guess what? I *did* do it: a year at UTI, studying automotive technology. Where the old man goes from here, we shall soon find out. I am on my way.

Me on graduation day!

Photo by Madi Ellis | madiellisphotography.com

EPILOGUE

It is 5:45 AM on a rainy Monday. A car is taking me to the airport for an early morning flight out of town. It has been several months since I graduated from UTI and it feels strange, and yet strangely familiar, to be up at this hour. Weeks after graduation, I continued to awaken at 4:15 AM—even if I did not set an alarm—as if the daily routine of waking up early for school had irrevocably changed my body's internal clock. At first, my wife, who has been an early riser her entire life, wondered aloud, "Why are you up at this hour? You should sleep in now that you don't have to go to class anymore." I did not know what to say to her. I couldn't help it: I was up. *There is no way I could go back to sleep now*, I thought. It was as if I had been transformed into a morning person.

Old habits die hard, but they can be changed. I eventually stopped waking up so early in the morning by staying up later and later at night. I even stayed up until midnight one night, just to prove to myself that I could still do it. I don't recall seeing midnight at any point during my year attending UTI, so it was definitely a challenge for me.

As the car headed towards the highway, I passed rows and rows of houses in my neighborhood. I chuckled to myself because the driver was taking the same route to the highway that I took every day I drove to UTI. He took the same shortcut around the shopping mall and gunned it to get through the same intersection where the light does not remain green for very long—the same as I had done on my way to school. Eventually, he reached the highway I used to take to UTI. But instead of going under the overpass and turning left to go south, he turned right to head north, towards the airport.

I glance at my phone. It is now 5:50 AM, the same time that Mr. M (the instructor from Basic Engines) enters the building to get ready for the morning's class, as I watched him do day after day after day. *He is probably still teaching Basic Engines*, I think. *I wonder what chapter they are covering today. I wonder if he is going to tease a student the way he teased Valdez (the butt of Mr. M's joke—"That's* **two** *infractions!"). I wonder if Mr. M still insists that no one say, "My bad."* I smile to myself, amazed that everything is still so fresh in my mind, as if I was still attending school.

I think about my year at UTI often, practically every day. So many courses, events, and people made a strong impression on me. And yes, I retained plenty of technical knowledge from my year at UTI. I have all of my course materials, my notes, and the big red Course Book in case I need to look anything up or be reminded of how a certain system on a car works. I'm no Master Tech, but I now know enough to ask the right questions. Friends and neighbors are not shy when seeking advice about their cars, asking me to diagnose what needs to be fixed, or asking whether I can help them with a repair.

I am not currently working as an auto technician. Given my status as a senior citizen and my wariness about the auto repair industry, I don't see myself working in a dealer or repair shop. While a student at UTI, I assiduously turned down all requests by the employment department to meet with prospective employers, even though on paper my grades and my attendance record made me a very desirable prospective employee. I felt it would be disingenuous for me to interview, even for practice, because I had a strong feeling I would not like working in a shop atmosphere or trying to beat the flat rate on every job. I know myself now. Witness the lab finals: I don't work well under time pressure, I overthink things, so what's the point? Even more importantly, I did not want to take away an employment opportunity from another student, who certainly needs the job more than I do.

But I do see myself getting involved in some aspect of the automobile industry, armed with the new knowledge that I now possess. Which is why I am on my way to the airport now. I am extremely interested in helping students who cannot afford to go to technical school overcome the financial challenges they face in order to get the training they need. It is expensive to attend technical school, especially UTI. I saw the economic hardships that students bore every day at UTI, and it had a profound impact on me. Even where the tuition cost of technical education is less, such as at a community college, the other "life happens" costs are daunting for many aspiring techs who desire an education. I want to help others, like the friends I made at UTI, attain their goal of becoming technicians in the transportation industry without incurring so much debt.

While at UTI, I came across a 501(c)(3) charitable organization, TechForce Foundation, that provides scholarship and grant money to aspiring technicians and champions them through their education. TechForce also has an initiative to encourage young women to enter the workforce and become technicians in the transportation industry. I could find no other charitable organization that does this type of outreach, so I became very attracted to TechForce as a result. From my year at UTI, I continue to ask myself, *What can I do to encourage young men and women to work in the auto tech industry? What can I do to lessen the financial burden they will incur and help them make smart decisions regarding their careers in the industry?* The work that TechForce is doing in this regard is a good start. Many large companies in the automobile industry, as well as high-net-worth individuals, celebrities, and industry leaders are engaged with or partner with TechForce and contribute to its efforts on an annual basis.

The reason for my trip out of town: I have been invited to meet with the CEO of TechForce and others involved in the organization to share my thoughts on current strategy, targets, and goals, as well as fundraising efforts. My background as a senior partner at an international law firm along with my experience attending UTI puts me in a unique position to add value. From my year at UTI, I saw firsthand the plight of many students who are struggling to make ends meet, who try to get by with little or no money, and who incur a great deal of debt to finance an education they see as a necessary path to a more secure financial future in an industry that attracts them. Almost all of my friends at UTI were in this boat. Short of paying their tuition bills myself, I am eager to find other ways to help them. And by that, I mean I am eager to support the ways in which TechForce can help them. In preparation for this meeting, I have already reviewed a lot of publicly available information about TechForce to gain some valuable background. I plan to review it again on the plane. I am armed with questions, which I am not afraid to ask the CEO. In this case, I don't think my questions will indicate that I am overthinking things. And luckily for me, following this meeting, there will be no 10-point test and no lab final. The next step begins with a conversation with the CEO. I can definitely handle this one.

And I plan to keep in touch with all of my UTI friends. It is the least I can do: follow their progress and careers and encourage them as much as possible. I have already exchanged several text messages with Rogers, Valdez, Gordon, and Alonzo. Rogers has a great job with an independent shop. Valdez got a job at a Lexus dealership. Gordon does not graduate from UTI until next year, and I will be there to cheer him on. After that, he will train with Mercedes Benz in Dallas. Alonzo graduates from the BMW STEP Program in a few weeks. I plan to be there for him, too. These guys are going to make it, I just know it.

But it is still early in the morning and, to quote Robert Frost,

"I have miles to go before I sleep." [46] I have miles to go before I get to the airport, too. The rain has slowed traffic to a crawl, and I expect my flight will be delayed. So I pull out my phone and begin scrolling through various apps and websites. Eventually, I end up going through my photos. To my surprise, I come across a screenshot of a Facebook post from the day I graduated from UTI. My daughter took a memorable photo of me in my graduation garb after the ceremony, with my arms raised in a victorious *"I did it!"* pose. Her Facebook post under the photo she took that day says it all:

> *This is so unbelievably cool! After 30+ years as a lawyer, my dad enrolled in Universal Technical Institute where he spent the past year learning everything he could about being an automotive tech and what it takes to work in the industry. Granted, no one is going to hire a 60 something year old as a mechanic at a Lexus dealership, but acquiring the same knowledge as a professional is all my dad ever wanted. There is no end to learning and you can 100% teach an old dog new tricks. Congratulations, Pop, I'm so so SO incredibly proud of you. Can't wait to see what you do next.*

---

46   Robert Frost, "Stopping by Woods on a Snowy Evening," 1923.

THANK YOU FOR READING

Thank you so much for choosing to take this journey with me. I am glad that you stopped by.

Please don't hesitate to reach out if you have any questions about my book, or to share your own industry experience and journey with me.

I enjoy connecting with readers and would be happy to hear from you.

You can email me at davidbook911@gmail.com.

Thanks again,

–David

A QUICK FAVOR PLEASE?

Before you go, can I ask you for a quick favor?

Good, I knew I could count on you.

Please take a quick minute to go to Amazon and leave this book an honest review. I promise it doesn't take very long, but it can help this book reach more readers just like you.

Thank you so much for reading.

–David

ABOUT THE AUTHOR

Photo by Madi Ellis | madiellisphotography.com

David W. Ellis spent more than 37 years counseling multinational companies on international employment and benefits issues. He retired early from a successful law practice to pursue his passion: cars. David resides in Chicago, Illinois, with his wife and is the resident car guy for his family, friends, and neighbors.

Made in the USA
Coppell, TX
26 May 2020